SpringerBriefs in Economics

SpringerBriefs present concise summaries of cutting-edge research and practical applications across a wide spectrum of fields. Featuring compact volumes of 50 to 125 pages, the series covers a range of content from professional to academic. Typical topics might include:

- A timely report of state-of-the art analytical techniques
- A bridge between new research results, as published in journal articles, and a contextual literature review
- A snapshot of a hot or emerging topic
- An in-depth case study or clinical example
- A presentation of core concepts that students must understand in order to make independent contributions

SpringerBriefs in Economics showcase emerging theory, empirical research, and practical application in microeconomics, macroeconomics, economic policy, public finance, econometrics, regional science, and related fields, from a global author community.

Briefs are characterized by fast, global electronic dissemination, standard publishing contracts, standardized manuscript preparation and formatting guidelines, and expedited production schedules.

Yoshikiyo Sakai

Deflation and Fiscal Deficits

Three Questions About Japanese Economic Policy

Springer

Yoshikiyo Sakai
Faculty of Economics
Kanagawa University
Yokohama, Kanagawa, Japan

ISSN 2191-5504 ISSN 2191-5512 (electronic)
SpringerBriefs in Economics
ISBN 978-981-97-0414-9 ISBN 978-981-97-0415-6 (eBook)
https://doi.org/10.1007/978-981-97-0415-6

This Springer imprint is published by the registered company Springer Nature Singapore Pte Ltd.
The registered company address is: 152 Beach Road, #21-01/04 Gateway East, Singapore 189721, Singapore

Paper in this product is recyclable.

Acknowledgements

This book is written in memory of the late Professor Masayuki Ohtaki.

I would like to express my gratitude to Prof. Kazumi Asako and the attendees for their comments at the seminar at Rissho University, and Prof. Katsuhito Iwai and the attendees for their comments at the seminar at Kanagawa University. I would also like to express my gratitude to Professor Neil Wallace for his comments during my overseas research at Penn State University. The author is solely responsible for the content of this research.

Contents

Chapter 1
Circumstances of Questions and Theoretical Background

Abstract In this study, we will focus on three problems related to the recent economic policy of Japan and present their answers. We will describe and analyze (i) what mechanism exists for fiscal and monetary policy and the price level, (ii) whether the modern monetary theory (MMT)proposition that public debt increases people's wealth and savings fits into the standard macro model, and (iii) whether Blanchard's assertion that budget deficits are net wealth in the US economy can be applied to Japan economy as well. The propositions of Sims' the fiscal theory of the price level (FTPL), Kelton's MMT, Japan's Ricardian type argument the so-called Crocodile Mouth theory, and Blanchard's non-Ricardian type of government have been understood as independent economic perceptions, but they will be shown as a theoretically coherent story.

We will choose 3 questions about the current economic policy of Japan and give theoretical answers on the base of macroeconomic framework. Japan's economic problem is characterized by countermeasures against deflation under massive fiscal deficits. To solve this problem, monetary policy has played a role in combating deflation under the ever-accumulating fiscal deficits. Therefore, if monetary policy alone cannot counteract deflation, the question of how to consider fiscal deficits will inevitably arise. For this analysis what is required is an economic model that clarifies the roles of the government that has the right to issue government bonds as well as tax collection and the central bank which has the right to issue currency. Furthermore, the relationship between fiscal deficits and fiscal collapse must be theoretically explained. The three problems and answers discussed in this research relate to these long-standing economic problems of Japan.

Question 1. Aiming at price stability belongs to one of the mandates by central banks. Does there exist any role of price level control played by the government (fiscal authority)?

Question 2. How to understand the modern monetary theory (MMT) claim, "fiscal deficits increase people's wealth and savings" from viewpoint of standard macroeconomic theory?

Y. Sakai, *Deflation and Fiscal Deficits*, SpringerBriefs in Economics,
https://doi.org/10.1007/978-981-97-0415-6_1

Question 3. The widespread notion is "public debt levels are too high and must urgently be decreased." Is public debt itself bad?

1.1 Countermeasures Against Deflation Under Massive Public Debt

With the bursting of the bubble that began in 1990, deflation occurred in the Japanese economy in 1997 and 98. Monetary policy was adopted as a measure against inflation in the United States in the 1980s, for example, but there was no precedent for monetary policy to be used as a measure against deflation.[1] As a result, the Bank of Japan had no choice but to develop policy management measures that were called unconventional. This is because, under conventional monetary policy, once the interest rate target was stuck at zero, there was no further monetary easing. This is named as "zero interest rate lower bound." Therefore, the deflationary countermeasures implemented by the Bank since 1998 have had a significant impact on monetary policies in each country in response to the Lehman shock in 2008.

The deflation caused Japan by the nonperforming loan problem of financial institutions that was caused by the collapse of land and stock prices seemed to have ended around 2006, but the economy faced deflation again. Signs of a global financial crisis began to appear around August 2007, but it was through the Lehman shock that the Japanese economy was directly affected. This research describes Japan deflation separately before and after the Lehman shock. Measures taken prior to the Lehman shock were probably due to the yen's depreciation policy through foreign exchange intervention under monetary easing, which contributed to economic recovery and price rises. On the other hand, against the deflation that occurred after the Lehman shock, the quantitative and qualitative monetary easing (QQE) in 2013 were implemented based on the belief that deflation was a monetary phenomenon. It meant that deflation could be resolved by monetary policy. Therefore, the series of QQE implemented under accumulating public debt were a policy experiment to verify how much deflation could be dealt with by monetary policy alone.[2]

The three types of QQE mechanisms introduced under the inflation target (price stability target of 2 percent) since 2013 mainly consist of two components: controlling interest rates through operations and inflation expectations. Evaluating these economic conducts of monetary policy and their experience, we find, firstly, that not only short-term interest rates but also medium- to long-term interest rates can be manipulated by operations. Starting with guiding short-term interest rates to zero percent, the Bank gradually became conscious of lowering medium- to long-term

[1] In the United States in the 1980s, when P. Volcker was chairman of the Federal Reserve, countermeasures against inflation were implemented with a target value for the money supply.

[2] Here, the series of QQEs refers to three types: QQE introduced in 2013 and QQE with a Negative Interest Rate and QQE with Yield Curve Control introduced in 2016.

interest rates, flattening and shifting downward the yield curve, and finally succeeded in shaping the whole yield curve.

The concept of inflation expectations constitutes another component of QQE. Inflation expectations are "the inflation rate that people expect," and QQE states that they will be raised by strong and clear commitment made by the central bank to achieve the price stability target of 2 percent. Prior to QQE, it was announced as a time duration policy that promised the market the duration of the interest rate easing policy and gave the market credibility of the policy, for example the quantitative easing (QE) between 2001 and 2006. It was also a policy tool implicitly aimed at raising inflation expectations although the word of inflation expectations was not used.

QQE as an unprecedented monetary policy maneuver in financial history was successful for the first year of its introduction However, it was undermined by the consumption tax hike in April 2014. Subsequent additional measures, such as negative interest rates and controlling short- and long-term interest rates, could not achieve the inflation target. This suggests that inflation expectations are unlikely to recover once they decline. This is because financial markets not only react to monetary policy, but also to fiscal policy at the same time.

When inflation targeting became difficult to achieve, the fiscal theory of the price level (FTPL) and MMT came into the spotlight.[3] Both were policy proposals from the perspective of eliminating deflation through fiscal policy. One of the objectives of this study is to create a policy framework that contributes to countering deflation without contradicting the FTPL and MMT arguments.

While Japan implemented unprecedented monetary easing, active fiscal spending was not implemented to combat deflation because public debt had accumulated and increased. In the case the fiscal deficit is huge, fiscal spending and public debt are two sides of the same coin. In response, however Blanchard (2019, 2023) argues that public debt contributes to economic efficiency. Would there be consistency in these conflicting claims? To answer this question, this study will theoretically derive the relationship between public debt and financial collapse. This is because unless this relationship is clarified, there will be no conclusion on whether fiscal spending is possible in the economy.

1.2 Background of Fiscal Theory of Price Level

Let us explain the theoretical background of these three problems. Question 1 is concerned with FTPL which has come into spotlight after 2016, when the effects of QQE with Yield Curve Control, which was introduced in September 2016 with the

[3] Each Policy Board member's CPI (less fresh food) projections are published quarterly as Price Forecasts of the Majority of the Policy Board Members in the Outlook for Economic Activity and Prices. The postponement of achievement forecasts observed during this period is synonymous with a decline in inflation expectations from the perspective of policy mechanisms.

price stability target of 2 percent, began to show its limits. In other words, monetary policy alone could not achieve the inflation target, and it was necessary to consider the trying to find a way by fiscal policy. In particular, the lecture of Jackson Hole Economic Policy Symposium by Sims (2016) was notable for Japan that was struggling to achieve the price stability target of 2 percent through monetary policy alone, as it talked about specific policies of central banks in each country during the global financial crisis. Sims (2013) claims that "fiscal and monetary policy are inseparably intertwined, and fiscal policy is the sole determinant of the price level."

FTPL presupposes the interdependence of fiscal and monetary policy. This research presents a trading mechanism consisting of macroeconomic model that includes the financial sector and derives Sims' (2013) proposition that "fiscal policy can be the sole determinant of the price level." While monetary policy is a measure to guide the private economy through the supply of the monetary base as well as the interest rate policy, fiscal policy is a policy that proactively increases the money stock. FTPL is a mechanism that integrates these two policies. In other words, FTPL is a study that explores the mechanism by which fiscal policy controls prices within a framework that also incorporates financial transactions.

However, in Japan, discussions on FTPL have started from the perspective of whether fiscal stimulus is possible under huge public debt. In any case, during the period when QQEs were being implemented, the massive amount of public debt became a drag on fiscal spending, and fiscal stimulus as a measure against deflation was not adopted. In addition, the economic policy of Japan stipulated by Joint Statement of the Government and the Bank of Japan in 2013 that was designed based on a mechanism in which fiscal policy and monetary policy sought to achieve their respective goals independently of each other, i.e.., the Government establishing a sustainable fiscal structure and the Bank of Japan overcoming deflation. Series of QQEs have been implemented under this partnership.

Raising the consumption tax rate belongs to the Government's task to restore fiscal consolidation. If the consumption tax hike in April 2014 lowered inflation expectations, fiscal policy affected the central bank's inflation target. This case confirms Sims' assertion that fiscal and monetary policies must be established through an interdependent mechanism. Therefore, if inflation expectations did not work and deflation could not be eliminated by monetary policy alone, the problem lies in the policy framework itself.

If monetary policy could not have the effect of raising inflation expectations because of the consumption tax hike, how does fiscal policy relate to monetary policy and prices? The Joint Statement prevents us from reviewing this perspective. To illustrate this mechanism, this study will construct a macro-model framework that includes the sector of financial institutions, clarifying monetary base, money stock and government bonds.

In doing so, we will consider distinguishing between government bonds and the monetary base from the viewpoint of the economics of payments by Freeman (1996). The securities (IOU) issued by the government are government bonds, and the currency supplied by the central bank is the monetary base. From the perspective of theory of money, the difference between government bonds and the monetary base is that the former does not have the function of finality (payment completion), while the latter has.[4] Explicitly distinguishing between the functions of government bonds and the monetary base, we will construct a mechanism by which government spending increases the money stock. We will focus on payment service provided by the central bank. In other words, a macro-model designed on the economics of payment (see Fig. 5.2) will be used to analyze a trading mechanism by which fiscal policy can control prices.

1.3 Background of Modern Monetary Theory

The next thing to consider as Question 2 is how to think about public debt. MMT which favors fiscal deficits, is not written by standard macro models. We will consider the position of MMT within the framework of FTPL created to answer Question 1.[5] The most characteristic assumption of MMT would be that "expenditure precedes revenue" as government action, and the derived prominent proposition is "budget deficits increase the wealth and savings of the people." These claims are presented in Kelton's (2020) as Reality 1 as assumption and Reality 4 as its result. MMT is also a study that reinterprets the position of public debt from the perspective of theory of money. In other words, MMT argues that a state with the right to collect taxes and issue currency, unlike households, can determine expenditures before revenue, and that the government bonds (government liabilities) generated there can be regarded as assets if held by the private sector. Could the ideas of MMT really be coherent with theoretical macroeconomics? In this study, we consider whether MMT's arguments fit consistently within the framework presented to illustrate FTPL.

In advancing the analysis we will examine the case where the central bank directly underwrites government bonds (monetization) and the case where the government purchases government bonds after financial institutions have underwritten them. The former hypothetically assumes the policy conduct of the United States. On the other hand, during the period of a series of QQEs, the Bank purchased large amounts of JGBs, which has led to an enormous amount of current account balances held by financial institutions. Therefore, the latter assumes the case of Japan.

Kelton (2020) regards the monetary base and government bonds identical. Given such assumption, the proposition that "government sector liabilities (government bonds) are assets of the private sector" can be observed ex post facto in both cases.

---

[4] Payment means "to complete an economic transaction by paying some kind of consideration." Finality is a function to complete payment, and typical examples are the monetary base issued by the central bank and the demand deposits issued by financial institutions.

[5] Modern macro models such as DSGE (Dynamic Stochastic General Equilibrium) excel in economic analysis of dynamic causal relationships. MMT, on the other hand, is based on double-entry bookkeeping and the analysis is static. The lending relationship between the government and the central bank has not been analyzed in macro models. MMT's achievement is to shed light on this relationship.

We will show that the MMT assertion turns out a common phenomenon when the framework of macroeconomics is extended to the system including financial sector.

1.4 Background of Blanchard Assertion

The third question is related to the relationship between fiscal deficits and financial crisis.As an answer to Question 3, we will summarize different type of discussions about the fiscal deficits, keeping consistency with the set-up and assumptions in the answers to Question 1 and Question 2. Most of the opinion in Japan is that the economy, which is saddled with huge public debt, will collapse sooner or later and must be resolved immediately. In contrast, Blanchard (2019) even argues that public debt is net worth based on empirical analysis of the United States. The former is subject to a Ricardian-type government and the latter belongs to a non-Ricardian-type government. Do these claims conflict with each other? We will clarify that the two claims are not necessarily contradictory claims through a theoretical model that incorporates the assumptions of FTPL and MMT.

As the answer to the third question, we will present the model in which there is a threshold for public debt, and if public debt increases and exceeds the upper limit, the financial system collapses. In addition, it satisfies the claim by Blanchard (2019), i.e., within the realm of a budget deficit that follows a redeemable path, the greater the public debt, the more efficient the economy. Therefore, if it is within the threshold, a non-Ricardian argument is established, and if it exceeds the threshold, a Ricardian argument is established. It becomes clear that each claim looks at a model from a different perspective. This also explains why the government has repeatedly taken the action of new public debt in the middle of fiscal consolidation. Therefore, it will be important to find the threshold of public debt according to each physical environments of economies analyzed.

The set-up and results of this model are as follows. Since MMT denies commodity money and presupposes credit money, we will consider Question 3 in the overlapping generations model. In addition, we assume that the monetary base and government bonds are identical.[6] The equilibrium to be adopted is a sequence of temporary equilibrium which is evaluated by the Pareto criterion.[7] Then, we have obtained the proposition that the sequence of temporary equilibrium indicates that if the fiscal deficits do not exceed the upper limit, the issuance of new government bonds will increase the efficiency of the economy. On the other hand, if there is a threshold and the upper limit of the outstanding amount of government bonds is exceeded, the economy will collapse. Therefore, it becomes understandable in the model that the

[6] The reason for assuming the homogeneity of the monetary base and government bonds here is to maintain consistency with the answer to Question 2. As a result, the model belongs to the same class as the one by Sims (2013) and Blanchard (2019).

[7] While Blanchard (2019) conducts comparative static analysis, this paper conducts dynamic analysis by intertemporal equilibrium. Nor does Blanchard mention the mechanism of financial collapse.

conflicting claims about the public debt are only differences in analytical perspectives. The study of the threshold of public debt within the framework of the financial system will be a challenge for the future. Since this proposition obtained here is established under the assumption of MMT that the monetary base of MMT and government bonds are the same thing, it does not contradict the arguments in the answers to Question 1 and Question 2.

1.5 Structure of Research

To sum up, our research reconsiders each question from the perspective of Freeman's (1996) economics of payments in the framework of a macro model that includes financial institutions (see Fig. 5.2). We have analyzed the following topics, (i) a comparison between the independent policy alliance between the Government and the Bank of Japan (2013) and Sims' (2013) fiscal and monetary policy interdependence, (ii) the appearance of a proposition of Kelton (2020) as an ex-post phenomenon, (iii) the relationship between Crocodile Mouth Theory of public debt and Blanchard assertion (2020) under such assumption of government activity as spendings precede revenues. The difference of the assertions can be explained in the framework of ordinary macroeconomics. Therefore, the financial system presented here is a means of analyzing seemingly conflicting events and ideas from a unified perspective. The contents of this research are as follows. Chapter 2 provides a bird's-eye view of Japan's economic policies, which process has turned out a mixture of monetary easing and consumption tax hikes. In Chap. 3, we describe and analyze the structure of QQE and the Joint statement by the Government and the Bank of Japan in which monetary and fiscal policies are independent of each other. In Chap. 4 we describe the main assertions of FTPL and MMT respectively. Chapter 5 presents a macroeconomic framework that includes the financial sector and derives FTPL proposition from the interdependent fiscal and monetary policy. In addition, it is also shown this mechanism satisfies the claim of MMT. In Chap. 6, the propositions are presented such that while there is an upper limit of financial collapse to public debt, new debt (issuance of government bonds) turns out to increase economic efficiency if it is within the redemptive range. Therefore, the way of thinking about the fiscal deficits depends on whether it is within the range of redeemability of economies analyzed.

References

Bank of Japan. The "Price Stability Target" under the Framework for the Conduct of Monetary Policy. January 22, 2013.

Blanchard, Olivier. 2019. Public Debt and Low Interest Rates. American Economic Review 2019, 109(4): 1197–1229.

Blanchard, Olivier. 2023. Fiscal Policy under Low Interest Rates, MIT Press.

Freeman, Scott. 1996. "The payment system, liquidity, and rediscounting, " American Economic Review, Vol. 86, 1126–38.

Kelton, Stephanie. The Deficit Myth Modern Monetary Theory and the Birth of the People's Economy, Public Affairs. 2020.

Sims, A. Christopher. 2013. Paper Money. American Economic Review. 103(2): 563–584.

Sims, A. Christopher. 2016. Fiscal Policy, Monetary Policy and Central Bank Independence. Jackson Hole Economic Policy Symposium, Federal Reserve Bank of Kansas City.

Chapter 2
Timeline of Economic Policies in Japan

Abstract Chapter 2 provides an overview of the circumstances of measures by the Bank of Japan against deflation. Triggered by the bursting of the asset bubble that peaked in 1990, Japan's deflation occurred in 1997 and 1998. The Bank of Japan was forced to take unprecedented deflationary measures. The zero-interest rate policy and the quantitative easing (QE) policy were called unconventional monetary policy. The japanese economy, which seemed to have recovered through deflationary measures accompanied with time-duration effect, fell back into deflation due to the global financial crisis in September 2008. Quantitative and qualitative easing monetary policy (QQE) in April 2013 was a measure to achieve the 2 percent inflation target by judging that deflation is a monetary phenomenon. The 2 percent CPI estimate, however, started to falter since the consumption tax hike from 5 to 8 percent in April 2014. QQE with a negative Interest Rate in January 2016 and QQE with Yield Curve Control in September 2016 were announced, but these measures did not achieve the inflation target. On the other hand, the consumption tax rate was raised again from 8 to 10 percent in October 2019.

2.1 Emergence of Deflation in Japan

The three problems discussed in this research derive from the Japan economic problems of fiscal deficits and deflation and measures to address them. Let's start by explaining how the massive budget deficits, the chronic disease of the Japan economy, came about. Japan enjoyed high growth in the 1960s. However, the fixed exchange rate system (Bretton Woods System) collapsed due to the Nixon shock in 1971, shifting to the floating exchange rate system was shifted from 1973. As a result, the internationalization of the yen made it possible for companies to raise funds internationally. Furthermore, during this period, due to the lack of tax revenue caused by the first oil shock between 1973 and 1977, Japan was forced to issue a large amount of government bonds. This was the starting point that led to a cumulative increase in the Japan's budget deficit. On the other hand, the massive issuance of government bonds improved financial markets and created the soil for open market operations.

Y. Sakai, *Deflation and Fiscal Deficits*, SpringerBriefs in Economics,
https://doi.org/10.1007/978-981-97-0415-6_2

Also, during this period, the means of financing for the companies progressed from direct finance that dominated the postwar Japan, to indirect finance.

The Japanese economy, which successfully survived the second oil crisis between 1978 and 1983, maintained a period of stable growth until the mid-1980s. The economy was at its most prosperous in world history in the late 1980s. The Plaza Accord in 1985 had an intention that the U.S. economy which had twin deficits (current account deficits and budget deficits) under the Cold War was supported by the at-the-time strong economy of Japan and West Germany. During this period, the United States and the United Kingdom advocated small governments, and privatization of public works was active in Japan, so economic stimulus measures were taken through monetary easing rather than economic expansion through fiscal spending. Therefore, the bubble of Japan can be said to be the result of international cooperation. At that time, the main measure of monetary policy by the Bank was the official discount rate, and monetary easing was carried out by successive reductions in the official discount rate.

Under these circumstances, Black Monday in October 1987 forced the Bank to continue its accommodative policies.[1] Despite concerns about inflation due to excessive monetary easing, the Bank feared that a rate hike in Japan would trigger a recurrence of the global financial crisis. As a result, excess liquidity was left unattended in financial markets. However, contrary to the conventional wisdom that an increase in the money supply would inevitably lead to inflation, prices hardly increased, and instead only the prices of assets (land and stock prices) soared abnormally. A bubble is a phenomenon in which the price of a specific object rises rapidly and then collapses, deviating from the basic requirements (called fundamentals) based on the real economy. Therefore, the bubble and burst of the Japan that peaked in 1990 was a surge and crash in asset prices.

In Japan where direct taxes were the mainstream, a consumption tax with a tax rate of 3% was first introduced in April 1989 during the bubble economy.[2] Then, as a result of the collapse of asset values due to the total amount regulation of bank loans (1990–1991) and the land value tax (1992–1998) aimed at breaking the bubble, financial institutions became burdened with a large amount of nonperforming loans, and the Japan economy entered a long-term recession of the so-called "lost decade."[3] The non-performing loan problem in Japan was caused by excessive real estate loans by financial institutions.[4] The total amount regulation of bank loans was a guidance

---

[1] Black Monday was the first financial crisis since the end of World War II. However, unlike the subsequent financial crises, there were no non-performing loans held by financial institutions, nor was there a diffusion of risk through securitized products. Therefore, with a "crisis management system" providing a large amount of liquidity in financial markets, the Fed succeeded in ending the panic in a short period of time.

[2] After this, the consumption tax rate will be raised from 3 to 5% in 1997, from 5 to 8% in 2014, and from 8 to 10% in 2019. Each time it had a more negative impact on the economy than the policy authorities expected.

[3] The Japan depression finally bottomed out in 2002.

[4] The Japan financial crisis could be finally solved by injecting public funds directly into financial institutions. On the other hand, the U.S. financial crisis triggered by the Lehman shock in 2008

that requires the growth rate of loans to real estate to be lower than the growth rate of total loans by financial institutions.[5] Looking at monetary policy, the official discount rate was raised rapidly after the bubble that peaked in 1990, and then sharply lowered after the bubble burst.

At that time, there was a myth in the Japan that land prices would not fall, and credit creation consisted of loans secured by financial institutions using land as collateral. From the present point of view, the total amount regulation of bank loans can be said to be a policy that forcibly suspends credit creation. Moreover, the financial system was built on the myth that financial institutions would not fail. In other words, Japan had no legal mechanism to deal with financial institutions with nonperforming loans. The prudential policy was established in 1998 when the financial crisis occurred. On the other hand, in the financial system the interest rate liberalization was completed in 1994, and the Bank announced in 1995 that it would adopt the open market operation as its main monetary policy management. Therefore, after this, measures against deflation have been mainly implemented through fund-supplying operations.

The consumption tax rate was raised to 5% in April 1997 as part of fiscal structural reforms, as the Japan economy showed a temporary recovery trend despite a large amount of nonperforming loans remained unattended. The recovery of this period was called the "false dawn" later. However, in conjunction with the Asian currency crisis that occurred immediately afterward, Japanese economy fell into a circumstance of financial crisis. It is from this period that deflation manifested itself in Japan.

In the following, we will describe and evaluate the deflationary countermeasures in Japan divided into the periods before and after the Lehman shock. This is because the deflation before the global financial crisis was caused by an endogenous problem such as the bursting of the bubble in real estate prices and stock prices, while the cause of deflation after the crisis was an exogenous problem for the Japanese economy, which consisted of sluggish overseas economies and the appreciation of the yen. In the former as a countermeasure of deflation large-scale foreign exchange intervention was possible due to the favorable overseas economy. In contrast, foreign exchange intervention in the latter period aimed at depreciating the domestic currency was not acceptable in the circumstance of the global financial crisis. Therefore, the Bank became mainly responsible for countermeasures against deflation.

---

was an expansion of the crisis through securitized products. In the case of Japan nonperforming loans affected the real economy, while in the case of the United States credit instability in securities spreaded the crisis through financial markets. They are different in type.

[5] During this period, the guidance for financial institutions belonged to the Ministry of Finance. The separation of fiscal and monetary systems took place after the economy fell into a financial crisis in 1997, when authority for institutional design of the financial system was transferred to the Financial Services Agency. At present, monetary policy consists of institutional design managed by the Financial Services Agency and policy management by the Bank. The Bank of Japan Act was newly enacted in 1998, and the mechanism of policy conduct at that time was quite different from the present.

2.2 Deflationary Countermeasures Before the Lehman Shock

Japan deflation began with the financial crisis of 1997–1998. As a result, the Japan economy has had to deal with the complex problem of countermeasures against deflation under massive public debt. Japan also experienced the reality that the economic phenomenon of deflation lasted for a long time once it occurred. This is very different from the event in which inflation generated by the first oil shock subsided in a short period of time and stable growth was achieved thereafter. At that time, macroeconomic policies against inflation had been established, but there was no experience with measures against deflation. Therefore, the Bank was forced to devise unprecedented measures called unconventional monetary policy to combat deflation.

The biggest problem with deflation is that once short-term interest rate (call rate) is lowered to zero percent through operations, there is no room for further reductions, which is called the zero lower bound, and traditional monetary policy becomes ineffective. Therefore, promises about the duration and achievement of the policy were added to the means of policy announcement, and at the time of its introduction, it was called "policy duration effect."[6] After this, this class of deflationary countermeasures were called a policy framework because they were policy management measures that included not only policy goals but also commitments regarding the timing of policy achievement.

Let's start by reviewing the economic policies of Japan since the outbreak of deflation in Japan. The following Table 2.1 shows the fiscal and monetary policies of Japan since the outbreak of deflation in chronological order.

The zero-interest rate policy from 1999 to 2000 was the first attempt to combat deflation. The outline of the zero-interest rate policy was to guide the call rate to zero percent through operations, and to add a commitment that this easing policy would be continued "until deflationary concerns are dispelled." Prior to the onset of deflation, the Bank's monetary policy adopted a policy of setting a target value for the money market rate (call rate) and guiding it through operations. By this time the Bank's primary monetary policy had changed from official discount rates to operations, so measures to combat deflation would be addressed through fund-supplying operations.[7]

During the period under the zero-interest rate policy, the Japan economy was on a temporary recovery trend as legal arrangements for the disposal of failed financial institutions were in place and public funds were injected into financial institutions

---

[6] Since the Lehman shock, central banks around the world have adopted this type of policy management, so the policy duration effect is now called forward guidance. In any case, Japan's policy experience during this period has become the basis for subsequent deflationary countermeasures.

[7] The Bank has not changed its reserve requirement ratio since 1991. In addition, the official discount rate was renamed to the base discount rate and the basic loan rate, and the Bank lends to financial institutions that meet the conditions by the Lombard-Type Lending Facility, so since then the role of the Bank is to be a passive conduct.

Table 2.1 Timeline of fiscal and monetary policies in Japan

Year	Month	Day	Operating target	
1997	04	01	Consumption tax rate hike from 3 to 5%	R
1997 1998	09 12		Period of the financial crisis and the outbreak of deflation	R
1999 2000	02 08	12 11	Zero interest rate policy	R
2001 2006	03 03	19 09	Quantitative easing policy (It was also a time of large-scale foreign exchange intervention aimed at depreciating the yen.)	$R \Rightarrow Q$
2008	09	15	Lehman shock	
2010 2013	10 04	05 04	Comprehensive monetary easing	R
2013	01	22	The "price stability target" under the framework for the conduct of monetary policy Joint statement of the government and the bank of Japan on overcoming deflation and achieving sustainable monetary easing	
2013	04	04	Quantitative and qualitative monetary easing	$R \Rightarrow Q$
2014	04	01	Consumption tax rate hike from 5 to 8%	
2014	10	31	Expansion of the quantitative and qualitative monetary easing	Q
2016	01	09	Quantitative and qualitative monetary easing with a negative interest rate	Q
2016	09	21	Quantitative and qualitative monetary easing with yield curve control	$Q \Rightarrow R$
2018	07	31	Strengthening the framework for continuous powerful monetary easing	R
2019	10	01	Consumption tax rate hike from 8 to 10%	
2021	03	19	Further effective and sustainable monetary easing	R

Note The notation R means the period of the interest rates as the operating target while Q means the period of the quantity of monetary base as operating target. $R \Rightarrow Q$ means that the main operating target has been changed from interest rates to quantity of the monetary base. On the other hand, $Q \Rightarrow R$ means that the main operating target has been changed from quantity of the monetary base to interest rates

with nonperforming loans. Therefore, the zero-interest rate policy will be terminated after about one and a half years of implementation. At that time, there was no consensus that it would take a considerable amount of time from the onset of deflation to its end.

At the termination of the zero-interest rate policy in August 1999, there was a disagreement between the Policy Board and representatives from the government opposing the termination of the zero-interest rate policy at the Monetary Policy Meeting. This was the first time that the government presented a request to the Policy

Board to postpone the policy decision, and there have been no such cases since then.[8] The Bank were more worried about inflation caused by excessive monetary easing than about deflation. However, immediately after the end of the zero-interest rate policy deflation became more serious in the aftermath of the bursting of the IT bubble in 2000. Therefore, a stronger and clearer policy framework than the zero-interest rate policy was required.

The quantitative easing (QE) announced in March 2001 was a monetary easing policy that was implemented under the commitment to (i) change the operating target for money market operations from the call rate to the outstanding balance of the current accounts at the central bank, and (ii) continue the procedures until the year-on-year rate of change in CPI rises to zero percent or more in a stable manner.[9] In other words, the Bank had set a specific numerical target for the outstanding balance of current accounts at the Bank and pledged to continue operations to provide funds even if the call rate reached zero. For the first time, the policy tool was changed from interest rates (the target value of the call rate) to quantity (the amount outstanding of current accounts at the central bank). Furthermore, the Bank added a commitment through specific figure that the year-on-year rate of change in the consumer price index will continue until it reaches zero percent or more in a stable manner. Therefore, the Bank has indicated a clearer intention to ease monetary policy than the zero-interest rate policy.[10] At the end of QE in March 2006 the target value of the outstanding balance of the current accounts at the Bank had reached 30–35 trillion yen.[11]

At the same time as QE, the Japan government intervened in the foreign exchange by buying large amounts of dollars and selling yen to contribute to export industries. From the perspective of the international environment, the U.S. economy was amid a housing bond bubble, and the EU was also booming enjoying a bubble due to integration, so such foreign exchange intervention was easily tolerated. Therefore, the economic recovery during this period is considered to have been based on monetary easing to provide funds and the depreciation of the yen due to large-scale foreign exchange interventions.

In March 2006, the Bank lifted QE, announcing it had fulfilled the commitment to "continue the year-on-year rate of change in the consumer price index (less fresh food) until it reaches zero percent or more in a stable manner." At the same time, the Bank changed the operating target for money market operations from current accounts at the Bank to interest rate, stating that it would encourage the uncollateralized

---

[8] Decisions at the Monetary Policy Meeting are made by the deliberations of nine Policy Board members. Two government representatives can participate in the meeting, but they do not have the right to vote, only request the postponement of the proposed decision until the next meeting. At this time, the government's request to postpone the cancellation of the zero-interest rate policy was rejected by the committee, and then the decision to cancel the zero-interest rate policy was decided.

[9] Bank of Japan (2001).

[10] Since the announcement of QE in 2001, the attention has been paid to Outlook for Economic Activity and Prices, in which the Policy Board members publish forecasts of the economic growth rate and the CPI.

[11] Bank of Japan (2006).

overnight call rate to move at around zero percent. In other words, the Bank returned to a peacetime world of policy management in which short-term interest rates (call rate) is set and induced through operations.

During the period when QE was being implemented, there was criticism that even if the outstanding balance of central bank current accounts held by financial institutions was abundant, it only meant funds with zero interest rate remained in the Bank. However, at least QE had the effect of dispelling concerns that financial institutions' funds would short-circuit, and a financial crisis would occur.

On the other hand, the termination of the zero-interest rate policy in August 2000 and the introduction of the quantitative easing policy (QE) in March 2001 were implemented from monetary easing to tightening in a very short period. Although there was a bursting of the IT bubble between the two frameworks for the conduct of monetary policy, there was criticism that the zero-interest rate policy was lifted too early. From the implementation of such monetary policies, we can learn the rule of thumb that tightening from monetary easing should take as much time as possible and be cautious. Later, in dealing with the global financial crisis, the Fed tapered monetary easing off gradually for a very long time. Going back to Japan, monetary tightening was drastically carried out in a very short period against the bubble peak in 1990. These experiences suggest that if enough time had been spent implementing tightening, it would not have led to the sudden bursting of the bubble.

The conduct of monetary policy after QE is terminated consists of (1) Clarifying Price Stability, (2) Examining Economic Activity and Prices from Two Perspectives, and (3) Outlining the Current View on Monetary Policy.[12] The conduct of monetary policy announced at this time has become a standard for self-evaluating the subsequent monetary policy of the Bank. In (1), the nine Policy Board members, who are members of the Monetary Policy Meeting, expressed their "understanding of price stability", which is the understanding that prices have been stable in the medium to long term. At this point members agreed that the year-on-year rate of change in the CPI was around 0–2% would not differ significantly from the members' understanding of medium- to long-term price stability.[13] As to two perspectives, the first pillar was to examine whether prices would be sustained over the next one to two years, the second pillar would examine whether there was a risk of a bubble or financial crisis from a longer-term perspective, and (3) the two pillars would be to be examined in the Outlook for Economic Activity and Prices (Outlook Report). Therefore, since then, the forecasts of growth rate and price level and their risks of each Policy Board member can be obtained in concrete figures and charts. It can be said that the basics of the Bank of Japan's policy style were established at this point.[14]

---

[12] Bank of Japan (2006).

[13] The understanding of price stability was subsequently adopted as the commitment of the comprehensive monetary easing in 2010, changed its name to the price stability target in 2012, and finally reached the price stability target of 2% (inflation target) in 2013.

[14] The research on the relationship between the central bank and financial markets based on game theory has been actively conducted since the 1980s and practiced in the style of "dialogue with the market" since Greenspan's presidency of the Fed in 1987.

The nonperforming loan problem faced by financial institutions and deflation seemed to have been settled for the time being. There was criticism that QE was lifted too early, but the subsequent cost-push inflation suggests that the termination of QE at this time was appropriate. After this, the Bank of Japan gradually raised the target interest rate, which had been stuck at zero percent, and returned to its normal policy of guiding it through operations. The conduct of normal policy in peacetime means the establishment of dialogue between the central bank and financial markets through interest rate movements. CPI (less fresh food) revealed a rise due to soaring crude oil price until the Lehman shock in September 2008.

2.3 Deflationary Countermeasures After the Lehman Shock

With the outbreak of the Lehman shock the Japanese economy fell into deflation and recession again. Although the global financial crisis that followed the Lehman shock in September 2008 was not caused by problems of the Japanese economy, the overseas recession and the appreciation of the yen which was regarded as a relatively stable financial asset compared to the dollar and the euro, placed a heavy burden on the export industry. As a result, right amid the global financial crisis, it became difficult for the Japanese government to obtain an international consensus to intervene in the yen's depreciation anymore. In response to the appreciation of the yen caused by the drastic monetary easing policy adopted by central banks of other countries, the Bank was forced to implement stronger easing conducts, which was already accommodative due to deflationary countermeasures.

The policy framework for countermeasures against deflation implemented after the Lehman shock is comprehensive monetary easing between 2010 and 2013 and a series of Quantitative and Qualitative Monetary Easing (QQE) since 2013. Under comprehensive monetary easing, the Bank announced a virtually the zero-interest rate policy that would encourage the call rate to move at around 0–0.1 percent. Furthermore, as a commitment, the Bank introduced a time duration policy with the expression that the Bank will continue with the virtually zero-interest rate policy until "an understanding of medium- to long-term price stability" is achieved.[15]

The comprehensive monetary easing has since been criticized for being "too little and too late" because the effects of the policy were not noticeable. The reason for this was that it was introduced two years after the Lehman shock, and the initial response was delayed compared to crisis countermeasures in other countries, and the additional easing policies was introduced gradually. The content of stronger commitment was expressed little by little, for example in December 2009 for "clarification of understanding of medium- to long-term price stability" and February 2012 for "the goal of medium- to long-term price stability." Instead of setting a target value for current bank accounts at the Bank as in quantitative easing, the Bank continued

[15] Bank of Japan (2010).

to provide funds by setting a target value for call rate. In addition, the funds for operations would be presented separately from the balance sheet of the Bank. Compared to the policy of purchasing government bonds through QE operations, the means of presenting funds as asset purchase program had a weak policy impact on the market. It had not been learned that for additional easing to be effective in a deflationary economy, it is necessary to have the surprise effect of introducing easing conducts that at once exceed market expectations.[16] Until the end of 2012, the yen appreciated, and stock prices remained sluggish. The Japanese economy was in a state of deflation.

From now on, the main period covered by the analysis is the period from the announcement of the price stability target of 2 percent in 2013 to the onset of the pandemic in early 2020. Due to the outbreaks of the new coronavirus in early 2020 and of the war in Ukraine in February 2022 the Japan economy was shocked externally and fiscal and monetary policy was drastically transformed to cope with them. The focus of the discussion is on this period from 2013 to 2020 because it can be judged that policy effects are observed and evaluated in line with the actual situation when the economic environment was relatively stable.

In the series of QQE, the Bank conducted an unprecedented amount of JGB (Japanese Government Bond) purchases under the price stability target, setting the specific amounts for the provision of the monetary base. This policy framework was initially described as "deflation is a monetary phenomenon" based on the belief that deflation could be overcome by increasing the quantity of money supply. The basis for this is the inference that if the monetary base which is the currency supplied by the central bank, is increased by a large amount of funds supplying operation, the money stock will increase after a certain time lag and deflation will be eliminated. Namely, massive purchases of government bonds are intended to increase bank lending by lowering interest rates. Another key component is inflation expectations. Inflation expectations is the idea that if a central bank announces a clear inflation target and promises to achieve it, the market will act on the assumption of future inflation. Therefore, the achievement of the goal depends on the credibility on the central bank of the financial market. According to this conjecture, inflation target should be achieved if these two conditions are met. The details are analyzed below.

The transition of CPI (less fresh food) during the period of analysis (2013–2018) of this study is shown in Fig. 2.1. From the time-series trend of CPI (less fresh food), we can see the effects of introducing the three types of QQE mentioned below.

In January 2013 the price stability target of 2% year-on-year increase in the CPI was announced.[17] Inflation target has finally been achieved here.[18] The series of QQE is based on the inflation target as prerequisite. Starting with QQE introduced in

---

[16] One of the reasons why QE conducted between 2001 and 2006 was successful was the use of this surprise effect. The surprise effect at the introduction of monetary easing was maximized in the subsequent QQE.

[17] The joint statement by the government and the Bank of Japan, which will be described later, was also released at the same time as the inflation target.

[18] Until then, the term "understanding of price stability" or "price stability goal" was used, and here for the first time, the "price stability target" was clearly announced.

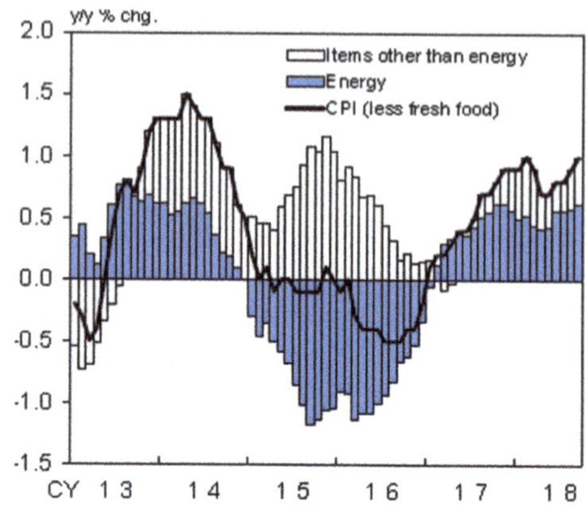

Fig. 2.1 CPI (less fresh food) between 2013 and 2018. *Source* Bank of Japan. Outlook for Economic Activity and Prices. July 2018, chart 42. *Notes* We cite the CPI (less fresh food) adopted by banks as their inflation target, but even CPI (less fresh food and energy) shows similar characteristics in shape

April 2013, the framework for the conduct of monetary policy were changed to QQE with a negative interest rate in January 2016 and QQE with Yield Curve Control in September 2016 by adding the new policy measures in order. From now on we will examine deflationary countermeasures with a view to QQE. The series of QQE and the consumption tax hikes are shown in Table 2.1.

QQE was announced in April 2013 under the commitment to implement operations that provide a large amount of funds until the inflation target of 2 percent is maintained in a stable manner "at the earliest possible time, with a time horizon of about two years."[19] As a quantitative component, the Bank changed its operating target from the interest rate (the uncollateralized overnight call rate) to the monetary base.[20] It was the adoption of the monetary base control. On the qualitative part, the Bank not only extended the average remaining maturity of JGBs from about three years to about seven years by purchasing JGBs, but also added securities containing risks. The extension of the average remaining maturity of JGBs is intended to shift the yield curve flat and downward overall.

To make this policy conduct possible, banknote rule and the asset purchase program introduced in comprehensive monetary easing were abolished. The banknote rule is a voluntary rule that limits the amount of government bonds that the Bank purchases from financial institutions to less than the outstanding of banknotes issued. The banknote rule was established in 2001 as a standard to prevent the purchase of government bonds from becoming monetary financing.[21] The abolition of the banknote rule enabled the Bank to purchase an unlimited number of government bonds through operations. After that, as you can see below QQE evolved as

[19] Bank of Japan (2013).

[20] In QE the outstanding balance of current accounts at the Bank is the numerical value of the operating target, but in QQE, it is the monetary base. The reason was that the monetary base was more understandable in terms of publication although the function from an economic policy point of view is the same.

[21] Monetary financing or monetization refers to the issuance of currency by a central bank to fund national finances.

a conduct for monetary easing against deflation, with a negative interest rates and with short- and long-term interest rate control, dependent on the situation that the achievement period of about two years becoming distant.

After the introduction of QQE, CPI (less fresh food) rose in the period, until the consumption tax hike from 5 to 8 percent in April 2014. After this, the inflation rate did not rise and QQE went astray. We have the fact that QQE was effective only in the first year, and since then the price stability target of 2 percent was not achieved. Suppose QQE were effective for one year but subsequently malfunctioned, the question is what the consumption tax hike did to the detriment of QQE mechanism. How would fiscal policy affect monetary policy? Is there any other way to restore the price stability target?

To overcome the sluggish price problem, the Bank introduced the expansion of QQE in October 2014, six months after the tax hike. This does not add new policy tools, but expands the scale of QQE (2013), and can be said to be the same in terms of framework.[22] Even with this policy, there were no signs of price rise. See Chart 1. Forced to extend the timing of achieving the inflation target, The Bank added to its original framework the QQE announced in 2013 by imposing a negative interest rate on a portion of current bank accounts at the central bank.

QQE with a Negative Interest Rate, announced in January 2016, imposed negative interest rate on current accounts held by financial institutions at the Bank in addition to QQE implemented in 2013.[23] It means for the Bank to lower the short end of the yield curve by slashing its deposit rate on current accounts into negative territory.[24] It was also intended to encourage financial institutions to lend by imposing some costs on current accounts at the central bank held by them. The introduction of negative interest rate was also a response to criticism that an increase in the current accounts at the central bank would not generate any profits, and therefore would be ineffective as a measure against deflation. The Bank obtained one more means for monetary easing by imposing a negative interest rate on current accounts at the central bank, in addition to increasing the supply of the monetary base and extending the average remaining maturity of JGB purchases.

How effective was QQE with a Negative Interest Rate? Even if the new means for monetary easing was added, the rise in CPI (less fresh food) did not appear. Therefore, the Bank self-evaluated its policy conduct of QQE as well as inflation targeting until that point and announced a new policy framework in September 2013 to add a measure to control the shape of the yield curve itself while maintaining negative interest rates.

QQE with Yield Curve Control (YCC), announced in September of the same year, maintained the framework of QQE with a Negative Interest Rate and added

---

[22] Bank of Japan (2014).

[23] Bank of Japan (2016).

[24] In particular, the Bank divides current accounts held by financial institutions at the Bank into three tiers (Policy-Rate Balances, Macro Add-on Balances, Basic Balances) and imposes a negative interest rate (minus 0. 1%) on the Policy-Rate Balance part. Other two are respectively imposed 0 and 0.1%. Therefore, a negative interest rate refers to only the application of minus 0.1% to the Policy-Rate Balances.

the overall shape of the yield curve as an operating target.[25] YCC consists of two components: "yield curve control" and "inflation-overshooting commitment." Yield curve control is a means by which the Bank determines the shape of the entire yield curve by purchasing government bonds with different maturity periods. Namely, in addition to setting the short-term rate at -0.1%, the Bank also adopted the operating target for the long-term interest rate as 0% JGB yields with a maturity of 10 years with the aim of flattening the yield curve and shifting it further downward. On the other hand, inflation-overshooting commitment is "expanding the monetary base until the year-on-year rate of increase in the observed CPI exceeds the price stability target of 2 percent and stays above the target in a stable manner." It aims to strengthen by the phrase "stays above the target in a stable manner" inflation expectations.

However, the decisive difference of YCC from previous QQEs is that the main operating target was changed from the amount of the monetary base to interest rates. The transition to YCC from QQE with a Negative Interest Rate means the end of policy conduct through "quantity."

At the time of the introduction of YCC, the Bank reviewed as comprehensive assessment the QQE from April 2013 to September 2016.[26] Here we will choose two contents of it which are related with our arguments. First, the analysis compares the cases of introduction of inflation targeting respectively and QQE to those without such measures by counterfactual analysis. Both reported that the policy measure influenced raising the price level. However, the price level employed in this analysis are CPI (less fresh food and energy), not CPI (less fresh food) which has been the target of the Bank. Second, it explained why inflation target had not been accomplished to that point. This part is associated with inflation expectations, which we will discuss in the following chapter.

The subsequent policy conducts were as below. The forward guidance for policy rates in "Strengthening the Framework for Continuous Powerful Monetary Easing," which came into effect in 2018, was to maintain the low levels of interest rates for an extended period of time as against the consumption tax hike scheduled for March 10, 2019.[27] In the Interest Scheme to Promote Lending of the "Further Effective and Sustainable Monetary Easing", which came into effect in 2021, consideration was shown for financial institutions whose profits were declining due to low interest rates.

The coronavirus pandemic, which occurred immediately after the consumption tax hike from 8 to 10 percent in October 2019, had an external impact on the economic environment of Japan. In addition, due to the global inflation caused by Russia's invasion of Ukraine in February 2022, shortages in the supply of grain and energy resources caused global inflation. The yen drastically depreciated due to the interest rate differential between Japan, which continued its low interest rate policy, and the United States, which raised interest rates as a measure against inflation, and the Japan economy was exposed to cost-push inflation.

---

[25] Bank of Japan (2016).

[26] Bank of Japan (2016).

[27] Bank of Japan (2018).

What impact did QQE have on areas other than financial markets? According to the Bank of Japan Act, its tasks are achieving price stability and the maintenance of stability of the financial system. On the other hand, price stability and maximum employment are the dual mandate for the Fed. In Japan, the unemployment rate has declined sharply since the introduction of QQE in 2013. Since the mission regarding employment is not legally required, its policy contributions to the labor market have been often overlooked, but according to the dual mandate, QQE can be evaluated as a result. However, this research will focus on the relationship between deflation and the inflation target.

References

Bank of Japan. New Procedures for Money Market Operations and Monetary Easing. March 19, 2001.

Bank of Japan. Change in the Guideline for Money Market Operations. March 9, 2006.

Bank of Japan. The Introduction of a New Framework for the Conduct of Monetary Policy. March 9, 2006.

Bank of Japan Comprehensive Monetary Easing. October 5, 2010.

Bank of Japan. Introduction of the "Quantitative and Qualitative Monetary Easing." April 4, 2013.

Bank of Japan. Expansion of the Quantitative and Qualitative Monetary Easing. October 31, 2014.

Bank of Japan. Introduction of "Quantitative and Qualitative Monetary Easing with a Negative Interest Rate." January 29, 2016.

Bank of Japan. New Framework for Strengthening Monetary Easing: "Quantitative and Qualitative Monetary Easing with Yield Curve Control." September 21, 2016.

Bank of Japan. Comprehensive Assessment: Developments in Economic Activity and Prices as well as Policy Effects since the Introduction of Quantitative and Qualitative Monetary Easing (QQE). September 21, 2016.

Bank of Japan. Strengthening the Framework for Continuous Powerful Monetary Easing. July 31, 2018.

Chapter 3
Structure of Quantitative and Qualitative Monetary Easing and Joint Statement with Government

Abstract A series of quantitative and qualitative monetary easing consists of interest rate control and inflation expectations. In the former, the Bank of Japan has gained the knowledge that the yield curve can be controlled by operations. As to the latter, it is recognized that inflation expectations must work for the quantitative and qualitative monetary easing (QQE) mechanism to be established. On the other hand, the government has set a goal of restoring fiscal soundness. Then, what is the relationship between monetary policy and fiscal policy? The economic policy of Japan has been governed by the Joint Statement of the Government and the Bank of Japan released in January 2013. Under this framework the Bank of Japan is responsible for achieving price stability of 2 percent, and the Government is responsible for sustainable economic growth with the aim of restoring fiscal consolidation. The characteristic of this statement is that each of them is independently responsible for the realization of the matters under their jurisdiction.

3.1 Effectiveness of Interest Rate Policy

Apart from purchases of risky financial instruments, the Bank's series of deflationary measures in particular the quantitative and qualitative monetary easing (QQE) consists of interest rate control through fund-supplying operations and measures to stimulate inflation expectations. Two operating targets will be paid attention in the following arguments. We will describe how interest rate policy as a measure against deflation has affected the yield curve first. Then we will explain what role inflation expectations were assumed to play in the QQE mechanism and why inflation expectations did not work.

Let us examine the evolution of monetary policy by operating targets from the perspective of the yield curve as a measure against deflation. Figure 3.1 shows the series of deflationary measures taken by the Bank of Japan in the form of yield curve. In zero-interest rate policy between 1999 and 2000, only short-term interest rate was operated with 0 percent, but the quantitative easing policy (QE) between 2001 and 2006 continued fund-supplying operation by setting a target value for

Y. Sakai, *Deflation and Fiscal Deficits*, SpringerBriefs in Economics,
https://doi.org/10.1007/978-981-97-0415-6_3

current accounts at the Bank of Japan even if the call rate was zero. Eventually, the operating target evolved from extending the average maturity of government bonds through a series of QQE in 2013 to form the overall yield curve. Namely, in April 2013, QQE shifted the overall yield curve downward under the inflation targeting by purchasing large amounts of medium- to long-term government bonds. At this point, the operating target was changed from interest rate (call rate) to quantity (monetary base), so the call rate, which is the origin of the horizontal axis, stuck to zero. Then, in January 2016, the Bank imposed a negative interest rate of 0.1 percent on a portion of current account at the Bank of Japan called by policy interest rate balance. Furthermore, in September of the same year, the Bank decided to purchase 10-year JGBs until their yields reached 0 percent.

As a result of the policy experiments, we gained the knowledge that not only short-term but also medium- to long-term interest rates, that is, the shape of the yield curve, can be formed through operations through a series of QQEs. In fact, the Bank succeeded in forming the overall yield curve by fixing interest rate of minus 0.1 percent for short-term interest rates and as an operating target purchasing 10 years JGBs at around 0 percent. It seems that the series of QQEs as a policy experiment can be considered complete at the stage of yield curve control. It was made possible largely by the knowledge that central banks around the world could purchase a variety

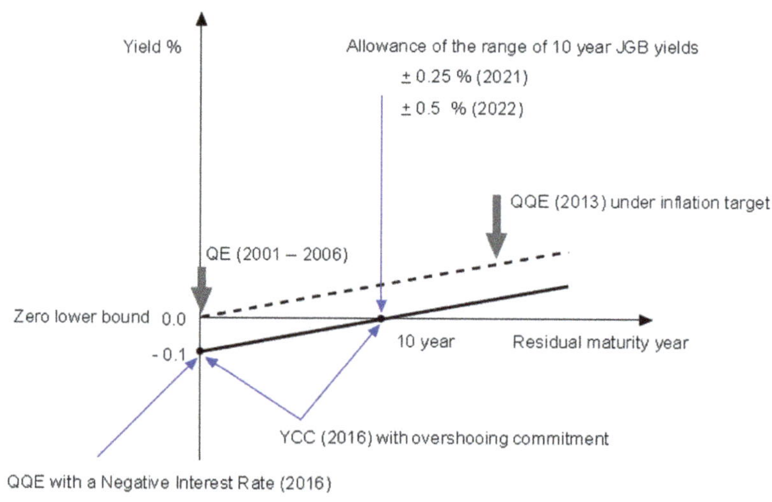

Fig. 3.1 Series of policy tools imposed on yield curve. *Notes* (i) QE (2001–2006) set an operating target for the outstanding balance of current accounts held by financial institutions at the Bank of Japan, aiming to shift the yield curve downward, mainly through short-term government bonds. (ii) QQE (2013) tried to flatten the yield curve through medium- to long-term government bond purchases under inflation target. (iii) QQE with a Negative Interest Rate (2016) imposed a negative interest rate (−0.1%) on a portion of current accounts at the Bank, and (iv) QQE with yield curve control (YCC) in 2016 attempted to form the overall yield curve by the operating target as the 10-year government bond yield rate (0%). Subsequently, (v) the range of fluctuations in the yields of 10 years JGBs was given to the financial markets in consideration of their functioning

of risky bonds during the global financial crisis, resulting in the ability to manipulate medium- to long-term interest rates. Namely, one of two major components, yield curve control can be accomplished as an experiment in monetary policy.[1]

After YCC, the Bank has given the yield curve the range of fluctuations from the target level 0% in long-term interest rate because it controls the yield curve flexibly. Specifically, the range of 10-year JGB yield fluctuations expanded to around $\pm$ 0.25% in 2021 and around $\pm$ 0.5% in 2022.[2] A conduct that allows long-term interest rates to fluctuate is, from a different perspective, allowing long-term interest rates to rise. Setting as operating target long-term interest rate at zero percent in YCC is clearly a measure against deflation. On the other hand, when the market demand for funds is high, if long-term interest rates are permissible up to the upper limit, an expansion of the range of fluctuations has the meaning of steepening the yield curve and shifting upward. Therefore, the expansion of the allowance of the range of 10-year JGB yields can be seen as a retreat from measures that are purely deflationary in mind.[3]

3.2 Effectiveness of Inflation Expectations

What about inflation expectations, which is another operating target against deflation? If we could obtain a rule of thumb that control short- and long-term interest rates can be achieved by purchasing government bonds, it is necessary to examine inflation expectations, which is another factor in achieving the price stability target of 2 percent. Let us now analyze the discussion from the perspective of inflation expectations, which are the basis of forward guidance. The target values for current deposits of the Bank by QE, inflation targeting by QQE and inflation-overshooting commitment by YCC are all promises to the financial market and operating targets that are expected to have the effect of commitments. Through a series of QQEs the common driving force of these measures is inflation expectations. It was at the introduction of QQE that the concept of inflation expectations was explicitly incorporated into the policy framework by setting a deadline for achieving the inflation target.

Figure 3.2, taken from Kuroda (2016), depicts the mechanism of QQE.[4] Inflation expectations derived from Fisher equation form the basis of the mechanism. Here, nominal interest rates are interest rates established in the financial market, and real

---

[1] QQE with yield curve control had a meaning as a countermeasure to deflation until Russia's invasion of Ukraine began in 2022. From this point on, however the phenomenon of cost-push inflation appeared due to shortages of energy resources and grains. As we mentioned, the range of fluctuations in long-term interest rate (10-year JGB yield) in the yield curve transforms into a means of monetary tightening.

[2] Bank of Japan (2021, 2022).

[3] Whether or not conduct which uses not only short-term interest rates but also long-term interest rates as operating targets, is effective as a measure against inflation would remain an issue for the future.

[4] Kuroda (2016).

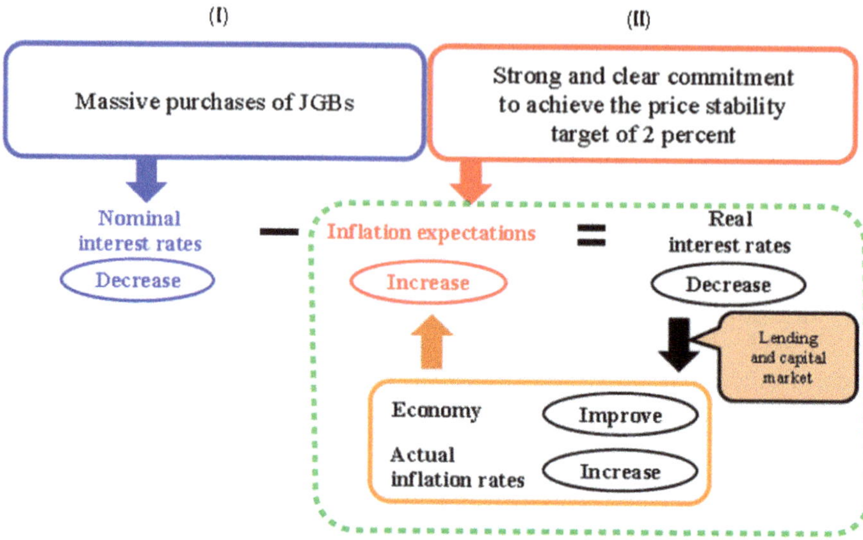

Fig. 3.2 Mechanism of "quantitative and qualitative monetary easing" *Source* Kuroda (2016). The battle against deflation: the evolution of monetary policy and Japan's experience. speech at Columbia university. *Notes* Notations (I), (II) and a green dashed rectangle are added by the author. From a series of QQEs experiments, we have gained a rule of thumb that nominal interest rates can be controlled by operations. In other words, the part (I) was found to be operable. Therefore, whether the mechanism works depends on inflation expectations, the part (II)

interest rates are interest rates that economic agents receive in conducting economic activities. For the economy to recover, it is necessary above all to overcome deflation by lowering real interest rates. If real interest rates decline, lending through financial institutions will be stimulated. In other words, the money stock increases and prices rise. As a result, the cycle depicted in the part of (II) on the right side of Fig. 3.2 will function, and a green cycle including the real economy will be established. Inflation expectations are impetus to mechanism of QQE.

To lower real interest rates in the equation shown in Fig. 3.2, it is necessary to lower nominal interest rates through large purchases of government bonds and to raise inflation expectations with a strong commitment to the price stability target of 2%. As we validated as to the yield curve control, we obtained a rule of thumb that allows short- and long-term nominal interest rates to be lowered through large-scale operations. Therefore, the Bank succeeded in lowering nominal interest rates by massive purchases of JGBS, which means the part (I) of Fig. 3.2 could work. In contrast, CPI (less fresh food) rose since the publication of QQE in April 2013. But it has begun to stray since the time of the consumption tax hike (from 5 to 8%) in April 2014. Later, even with inflation-overshooting commitment in 2016, the price stability target was not achieved. What would be the cause of this?

The Bank's explanation for the failure to raise inflation expectations is as follows: "Inflation expectations are formed through a combination of two components: a forward-looking component formed by the price stability target set by the central bank; and a backward-looking, or adaptive, component reflecting the observed inflation rate."[5] It is argued that QQE's failure to achieve the price stability target of 2 percent (inflation target) is due to the fact that the financial market was dominated by a backward expectation based on prolonged experience of deflation and could not exceed the forward-looking component intended by monetary policy.

If so, how does the Bank explain the rise in prices from April 2013 to April 2014, when QQE was introduced? If the Bank's thinking is to be consistent with two contradictory facts, it will be necessary to explain not only when it became difficult to achieve the inflation target since April 2014, but also when QQE achieved results. In other words, if a forward-looking component was large enough to outperform a backward-looking component only during this period between 2013 and 2014, and CPI (less fresh food) rose by positive inflation expectations, it must be explained what undermined the credibility of intentions by the Bank in April 2014. In this study, we think that the following inference is more reasonable. It is true that between 2013 and 2014 unprecedented large-scale easing was introduced. Furthermore, its surprise effect on the financial market was so great that it was called a policy of another dimension policy. If QQE's impetus is inflation expectations, however, the cause must be sought by the commitment itself. If we consider economic policy as a game theory between the policy maker and the private economy, the commitment in January 2013 Joint Statement of the Government and the Bank of Japan, "The Bank will pursue monetary easing and aim to achieve this target at the earliest possible time" was crucial.[6] It was announced in more explicit statement in April 2013 Introduction of the QQE, "The Bank will achieve the price stability target of 2 percent in terms of the year-on-year rate of change in the consumer price index (CPI) at the earliest possible time, with a time horizon of about two years."[7] In both cases, the commitment clearly stated the period until the policy was realized.

It could be considered, however, that the consumption tax hike from 5 to 8% in April 2014 has undermined the inflation expectations. This is because market perception of economic policy is influenced not only by monetary policy but also by fiscal policy. If inflation expectations are not expected to rise, the economic recovery and the rise in real inflation will not work, and the QQE mechanism will not function.

The subsequent strengthening of QQE in September 2014, QQE with a negative interest rate in January 2016, and QQE with yield curve control's overshooting commitment failed to recover expectations that had once been lost. This can be understood to explain that CPI rose for one year after the introduction of QQE in April 2013, and then did not rise even after exhausting measures. This trend can also be confirmed by the shape of the chart of break-even inflation, which is a proxy variable for inflation expectations. See Fig. 3.3. The findings suggest that inflation expectations with surprises may succeed in the first introduction but will not recover once impaired.

---

[5] See Bank of Japan (2016), Comprehensive Assessment, page 5.

[6] Cabinet Office (2013).

[7] Bank of Japan (2013).

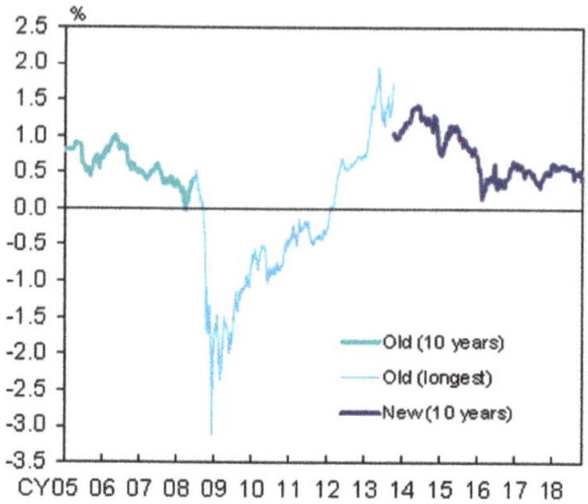

Fig. 3.3 Inflation expectations (BEI: Break-Even Inflation) Source: Bloomberg. Bank of Japan (2020), chart 40. *Notes* BEI (break-even inflation) rates are yield spreads between fixed-rate coupon-bearing JGBs and inflation-indexed JGBs. Inflation-indexed JGBs issued since October 2013 are designated as "new," while the rest are designated as "old." Figures for "old (longest)" are calculated using yield data for issue No. 16 of inflation-indexed JGBs, which matured in June 2018

This chapter has examined the two operating targets of QQE. Regarding the effectiveness of interest rate control, it became clear that the Bank could control the overall form of the yield curve since the Bank could control long-term interest rates through the operation. On the other hand, regarding the effectiveness of inflation expectations, it would be difficult to regain the effects of inflation expectations once lost. This also suggests that consumption tax hike seriously influences achieving the monetary policy of an inflation target. Financial markets consider not only monetary policy but also fiscal policy at the same time. Therefore, the solution to the problem is not to rely on inflation expectations, but to explore measures to influence prices, including fiscal policy. We will reconsider the relationship between fiscal policy and monetary policy within the framework of Japanese economic policy. Let us examine the mechanism of policy coordination between the Government and the Bank.

3.3 Joint Statement of the Government and the Bank of Japan

Joint Statement of the Government and the Bank of Japan was released on January 2, 2013. Since then, the fiscal and the monetary policy in Japan has been governed by this statement. Let us analyze the relationship between monetary and fiscal policy within a macroeconomic framework. Here's an excerpt of the division of roles from it.[8]

[8] Cabinet Office (2013).

The Bank of Japan: "the Bank sets the price stability target at 2 percent in terms of the year-on-year rate of change in the consumer price index. Under the price stability target specified above, the Bank will pursue monetary easing and aim to achieve this target at the earliest possible time."

The Government: "the Government will steadily promote measures aimed at establishing a sustainable fiscal structure with a view to ensuring the credibility of fiscal management."

In other words, the Bank will achieve the price stability target of 2 percent as soon as possible while the Government will be responsible for fiscal consolidation. A series of monetary policy developments and evaluations have already been explained. So, we will make clear here the background of fiscal policy and the relationship with monetary policy. Japan's fiscal policy belongs to Ricardian-type government on the premise of Ricardian effect. When public debt redemption is insufficient only in tax revenue, it is a Ricardian-type government that takes action to cover by future tax increases or expenditure reductions. According to Ricardian-type government, the action that the people suppress current consumption in consideration of the future tax hike is called Ricardian effect. Therefore, it is claimed that the first step in increasing future aggregate demand is to reduce current public debt by raising taxes or cutting expenditures. In fact, the Government has been aimed to reduce the accumulated public debt to achieve fiscal soundness. In Japan, public debt defined as government expenditure minus tax revenue, is often compared to a "crocodile mouth." The expansion of the budget deficit is called "the opening of the crocodile's mouth." It will sooner or later reduce to financial collapse If left unattended. Therefore, it is urgent for the Government to achieve tax consolidation through public debt reduction, even though the Bank has attempted to accomplish price stability of 2 percent by raising inflation expectations as well as massive purchases of JGBs.

As is apparent at first glance in Table 2.1, three monetary easing frameworks and two consumption tax hikes have been implemented in a mixed manner during since 2013. Here, the monetary easing framework refers to QQE in 2013, QQE with a negative interest rate and QQE with yield curve control in 2016. On the other hand, the consumption tax rate was raised from 5 to 8% in April 2014 and from 8 to 10% in October 2019. The reason why monetary easing policies and tax hikes were successively implemented was that the Japan economy was suffering from two compounds: the chronic disease of a huge fiscal deficit that was expanding, and the deflation that recurred after the Lehman shock in 2008.[9]

What have we learned so far from the verification as well as the explanation how things happened for this period? The interest rates can be controlled through operations. On the other hand, it is difficult to raise inflation expectations in a situation where the consumption tax rate is raised. This is because inflation expectations are

[9] The consumption tax (3%) was first introduced into the Japanese economy in 1989. It was two years before the bubble peaked in1990 burst. In addition, Japan deflation was triggered by the financial crisis in the fall of 1997 while the consumption tax hike (from 3 to 5%) had been implemented six months earlier, in April.

affected not only by monetary policy but also by fiscal policy.[10] Monetary policy alone cannot raise inflation expectations. It means QQE mechanism does not work, even if it is designed as a strong means of voluntarily increasing the money stock through credit creation. Therefore, to overcome deflation, instead of inflation expectations, we need means to increase exogenously the money stock.

What would be the problem with this policy combination? In the structure of the Joint Statement, the fiscal policy and the monetary policy set policy goals and measures independently of each other, and their policy mechanisms are separate. Figure 3.4 describes the partnership between the Government and the Bank of Japan. It does not consist of an integrated model of fiscal and monetary policy. In Chap. 5, we will prove according to what happened after the Joint Statement the financial market should evaluate economic policy as an integrated manner, rather than regarding fiscal and monetary policy independently.

[10] If inflation expectations had risen during this period, real interest rate might have declined and business investment might have increased, resulting in a rise in prices.

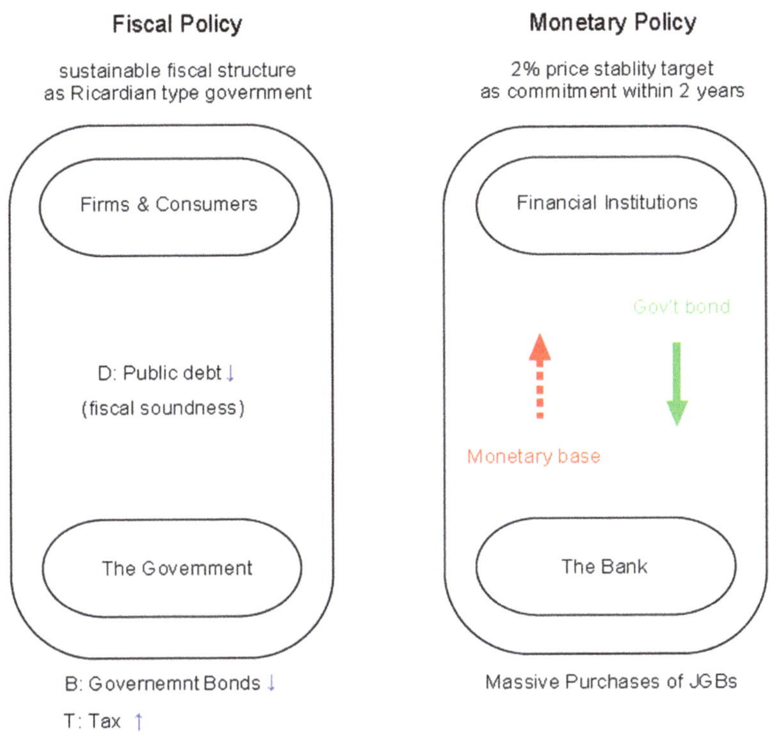

Fig. 3.4 Structure of joint statement of the government and the Bank of Japan. *Notes* The figure depicts that policy objectives and instruments for the Government and the Bank are independent. In fiscal policy, the government aims to reduce fiscal spending or raise taxes to restore fiscal soundness (reduce the outstanding amount of public debt). On the other hand, the Bank of Japan purchases a large amount of medium- to long-term government bonds under inflation target at the earliest possible time. The arrows depict the Bank's operations to purchase of government bonds by the monetary base

References

Cabinet Office, Ministry of Finance, Bank of Japan. Joint Statement of the Government and the Bank of Japan on Overcoming Deflation and Achieving Sustainable Economic Growth. January 22, 2013.

Bank of Japan. Comprehensive Assessment: Developments in Economic Activity and Prices as well as Policy Effects since the Introduction of Quantitative and Qualitative Monetary Easing (QQE). September 21, 2016.

Bank of Japan. Outlook for Economic Activity and Prices. July 2020.

Bank of Japan. Further Effective and Sustainable Monetary Easing. March 19, 2021.

Bank of Japan. Statement of Monetary Policy. December 20, 2022.

Bank of Japan. Introduction of the "Quantitative and Qualitative Monetary Easing." April 4, 2013.

Kuroda, H. 2016. The Battle Against Deflation: The Evolution of Monetary Policy and Japan's Experience. Speech at Columbia University. Bank of Japan.

Chapter 4
Fiscal Theory of Price Level and Modern Monetary Theory

Abstract Since around 2016, when it became difficult to achieve the price stability target of 2 percent through monetary policy alone, the fiscal theory of the price level (FTPL) and the modern monetary theory (MMT) have been attracting attention from the perspective of fiscal policy. Sims (2013) argues that fiscal and monetary policy consist of a single mechanism, and that fiscal policy is the sole determinant of price level. This is clearly different from the policy alliance between the Governments and the Bank of Japan. On the other hand, Kelton in her book "The Deficit Myth Modern Monetary Theory and the Birth of the People's Economy" (2020) derives the assertion that "public debt is the wealth of the state." It is contrary to the assertion that "the public debt is too big and will collapse sooner or later."

4.1 Fiscal Theory of Price Level

Since 2016, when the feasibility of the price stability target of 2 percent was shaken by monetary policy alone, the role of fiscal policy has been discussed.[1] We will now explain the fiscal theory of the price level (FTPL) related to the first question. The target paper is Sims (2013). Sims proposes FTPL by claiming two points about modern macro models in the following on page 563.

Point 1. "Conventional macro models with non-interest-bearing high-powered money, a money multiplier and a tight relation between the price level and quantity of money are inadequate as a framework for current policy discussion."

Point 2. "Fiscal policy and monetary policy are intertwined and tied together."

Then Sims asserts "FTPL integrates discussion of monetary and fiscal policy, recognizing that fiscal policy can be a determinant, or even the sole determinant of the price level." Let's explain each of points below. We are going to consider

[1] It was during this period that the already mentioned belief that "prices are a monetary phenomenon" began to crumble. After the consumption tax hike in April 2014, even if the rise in the CPI stalled, the Bank continued to resolve deflation through monetary policy alone until QQE with a negative interest rate in January 2016. However, with QQE with yield curve control in September 2016, the measures of monetary policy shifted from the quantity of the monetary base to interest rates.

Y. Sakai, *Deflation and Fiscal Deficits*, SpringerBriefs in Economics,
https://doi.org/10.1007/978-981-97-0415-6_4

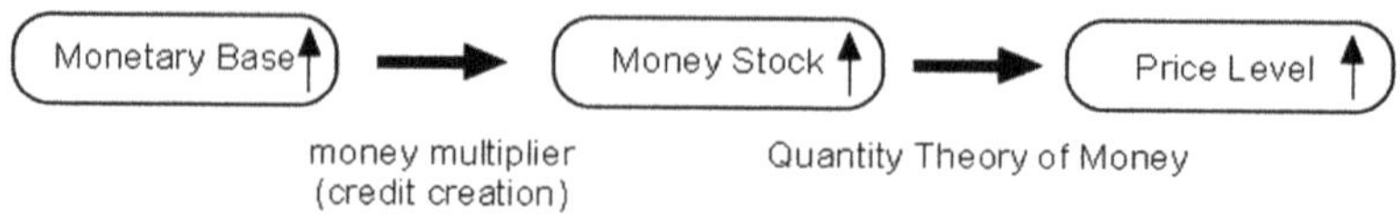

Fig. 4.1 Two-stage approach as conventional macro model. *Note* In traditional monetary theory, an increase in the monetary base leads to an increase in the money stock by money multiplier times, and then prices rise through the quantity theory of money

as to point 1 what exactly are conventional macro models. We quote the following sentence on page 582 from the conclusion by Sims (2013).

"The kinds of models that have been the staple of undergraduate macroeconomics teaching, with price level determined by balance between money supply and money demand, and money supply described using the money multiplier, are obsolete and provide little insight into the policy issues facing fiscal and monetary authorities in the last few years" on page 582.

The conventional monetary policy is based on the way of thinking that the supply of the monetary base would increase the money stock through an increase in bank lending, causing a rise in prices. We are going to interpret Sims' statement in the framework of so-called two-stage approach. The two-stage approach is a policy measure in which a central bank sets an interim target between a policy variable and the ultimate target. A typical framework described in Fig. 4.1 is to place the monetary base as policy means and use the interim target as the money stock to influence prices at the final target. Here, the relationship between the monetary base and the money stock is connected by money multiplier (credit creation), and when the central bank increases the monetary base, the money stock increases by that multiplier. Furthermore, if the money stock increases, prices will rise according to the quantity theory of money.

Central banks do not advocate this type of policy instruments today, but historically there was a case where Volcker's Fed set a target for the money stock in the 1980s. However, this was not a measure against modern deflation, but a policy aimed at calming inflation at that time. See Volcker and Harper (2018). On the other hand, behind the massive provision of the monetary base in the series of Quantitative and Qualitative Monetary Easing (QQE) that we have already explained, there is a belief that credit creation is expected to function and increase the money stock through a two-step approach. This is one of the reasons why the Bank of Japan provides a large monetary base through its operations in Fig. 3.4.

What was the reality in Japan? The series of monetary policies examined so far has shown that central banks can control not only short-term interest rates but also the shape of the yield curve itself by manipulating the monetary base. On the other hand, price stability of 2 percent was not achieved. This means that credit creation does not work, i.e., the money multiplier is not enough large to dispel deflation. Therefore, it is necessary to find a means to directly increase the money stock in financial markets where credit creation is not functioning.

As to point 2, we bring up two keywords of FTPL by Sims (2013) which are fiscal backup and nominal debt as fiscal cushion. Sims chooses three models to describe FTPL idea, (A) Samuelson's pure consumption loan model with storage, (B) fiscal backup for a Taylor rule, and (C) debt as a fiscal cushion. In A and B, it is argued that prices cannot be determined unless the government is given the right to collect taxes. This is a suggestion that tax revenues must be added to government budget constraints when we construct macro-models. In addition, in C's argument, it is claimed public debt acts as a cushion when controlling prices with public finances. It suggests public debt as another reason for existence of government bond market.

From these keywords, Sims (2013) on page 570 asserts the following. "A central bank, backed by a treasury that can run primary surpluses and issue nominal debt, is an ideal lender of last resort. Because it can create reserve money, it need never default. If it takes capital losses, and it is not backed by a fiscal authority, it could be forced to run a high inflation to restore its balance sheet, but this will not be a problem if it has fiscal backing."

Fiscal backup by government means the role of fiscal policy is to manage the public spending under arrangements of taxation and government borrowing. Nominal debt cushioning by the central bank means that central banks can purchase government bonds and provide an unlimited monetary base. It means that for the FTPL proposition to be established, the backup by the central bank is necessary. The central bank has the function as the lender of last resort not only to the financial institutions but also the government in some cases. It is understandable that the central bank can issue an infinite amount of central bank currency and purchase government bonds if inflation does not occur.

Let's consider the FTPL discussion in the framework of the two-step approach described above. Figure 4.1 depicted a mechanism in which the money stock increased through the functioning of credit creation by way of monetary policy. On the other hand, Fig. 4.2 describes a mechanism by which the money stock increases through fiscal backup and central bank purchases of government bonds. The inference is that fiscal policy affects the money stock and prices fluctuate. One of the candidates of this mechanism will be presented in Chap. 5 by constructing the framework of the financial system.

4.2 Modern Monetary Theory

Since monetary easing as a measure against deflation did not produce the expected results, fiscal policy as further deflationary countermeasures were considered, and the modern monetary theory (MMT) was another theory that came into the spotlight together with FTPL from around 2016. While FTPL was mainly a discussion with anti-deflationary measures in mind in Japan, MMT was paid attention to as the solution of the problem of the heavy public debt and its source of funding. Kelton (2020) takes the style of clarifying reality from the viewpoint of MMT, taking conventional

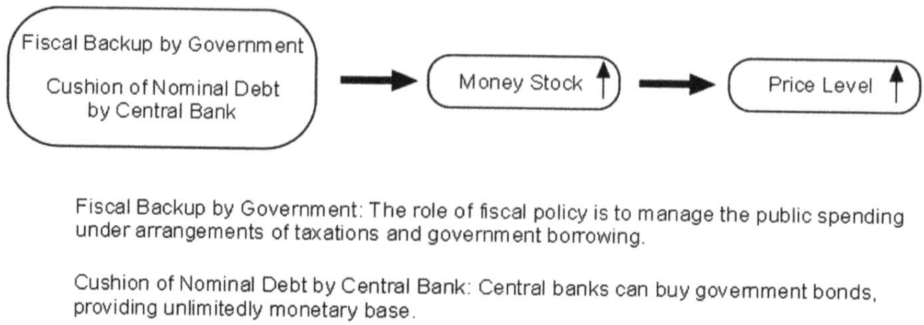

Fig. 4.2 Claim of FTPL. *Note* Fiscal backup by government and cushion of nominal debt by central bank determine the money supply

economic proposition as a myth. Here, we will consider one of the main propositions in the arguments of MMT. The proposition of MMT to be analyzed here is that "Fiscal deficits increase our wealth and collective savings."

Because the arguments of MMT are not described by the standard economic theory, we will proceed with the explanation to fit the framework of the model which will be created in the next chapter. To begin with, MMT sets up the economic system under credit money and monetary sovereignty, then the following hypotheses are imposed.

Hypothesis (i). S(TAB): Spending precedes taxing and borrowing.

Hypothesis (ii). Government bonds and the monetary base are taken identical.

Let's scrutinize each of them. By the notation of Kelton, S(TAB) means that spending precedes taxing and borrowing where S is spending, T is tax and B is borrowing, which is the claim as REALITY against MYTH #1. Kelton believes that in the conventional economic models the government presupposes the behavior of setting expenditures after obtaining revenue in advance, like households. Namely, the government behavior is represented as TAB (S) which means taxing and borrowing precede spending. It is in fact a proverb that "cut your coat according to your cloth." Contrary to this, Kelton asserts the real government can secure revenue after exercising its expenditures. The reason is that countries with monetary sovereignty have the power to collect taxes and can borrow through government bonds.

The second hypothesis is that the monetary base is equivalent to government bonds. The following is a quote on public debt from Kelton (2020) on page 36. "Then why does the government need to borrow? The answer is it doesn't. It chooses to offer people a different kind of government money, one that pays a bit of interest. In other words, US Treasuries are just interest-bearing dollars. To buy some of those interest-bearing dollars from the government, you first need the government's currency. We might call the former "yellow dollars" and the latter "green dollars."

The paragraph presupposes that a central bank that can issue an infinite amount of central bank currency (the monetary base) can purchase government bonds without restriction. It implies that the central bank is merely a permanent facility for returning public debt to the central bank currency.[2] From these hypotheses, Kelton derives the following proposition as REALTY, i.e., as a rebuttal against MYTH #4.

MYTH #4: Government deficits crowd out private investment, making us poorer.

REALITY: Fiscal deficits increase our wealth and collective savings.

Kelton particularly demonstrates this proposition via the following formula on page 106.

$$\text{Government financial balance} + \text{Nongovernment financial balance} = \text{Zero},$$

which is equivalent to

$$\text{Government deficit} = \text{Nongovernment surplus},$$

which means "the government's fiscal deficit is mirrored by an equal and opposite financial surplus in the nongovernment part of our economy" on page 107.

In other words, the government expenditure (liabilities) can be regarded as the private income (assets). We will construct a financial system which is consistent with this statement in the following chapter.

References

Kelton, Stephanie. The Deficit Myth Modern Monetary Theory and the Birth of the People's Economy, Public Affairs. 2020.

Sims, A. Christopher. 2013. Paper Money. American Economic Review.103(2): 563–584.

Volcker, Paul A. and Christine Harper. Keeping At It: The Quest for Sound Money and Good Government. Public Affairs. 2018.

[2] See the argument of public debt as a cushion on page 577–582 by Sims (2013).

Chapter 5
Answers to Questions 1 and 2: Financial System from Viewpoint of Payment

Abstract We give answers to questions 1 and 2, which are based on the discussions of the fiscal theory of the price level (FTPL) and the modern monetary theory (MMT). Specifically, from the perspective of economics of payments by Freeman (1996), we present a model consistent with the FTPL assertion that fiscal and monetary policy are intertwined. This mechanism explains the process by which the central bank underwrites government bonds, which are the source of fiscal spending, thereby increasing the money stock and consequently affecting prices. In addition, the MMT proposition "budget deficits are national wealth" is established between the public sector and the private sector from the assumptions, (i) the government activity in which revenue is financed after spending decision is made and (ii) government bonds and the monetary base are treated identically.

Question 1. Aiming at price stability belongs to one of the mandates by central banks. Does there exist any role of price level control played by the government (fiscal authority)?

Question 2. How to understand the modern monetary theory (MMT) claim, "fiscal deficits increase people's wealth and savings" within the macroeconomic framework?

Based on the previous discussions, we will give answers to questions 1 and 2. In the following procedure we will design the macroeconomic framework, incorporating financial institutions with the payment system according to the roles of the monetary base and the money stock. As to the first question, when the government makes expenditures funded by public borrowing, we will consider the case in which the central bank directly accepts government bonds and the other case in which private financial institutions accept them. In both cases, the argument of fiscal theory of the price level (FTPL) that fiscal and monetary policies are inseparably linked, and that fiscal policy is the determinant of prices, can hold. However, the model presented here only presents one of the mechanisms from which the claim of FTPL can be derived. As an answer to the second question, it is shown that suppose the structure of the financial system established here is viewed as an ex-post phenomenon, we can observe the MMT proposition that "an increase in national debt is an increase in private wealth" in both cases.

Y. Sakai, *Deflation and Fiscal Deficits*, SpringerBriefs in Economics,
https://doi.org/10.1007/978-981-97-0415-6_5

5.1 Financial System

We will construct the financial system comprises of the public sector and the private sector. The public sector consists of the government managing the fiscal policy and the central bank doing the monetary policy. The private sector consists of consumers, firms, and the financial institutions. The structure is depicted in Fig. 5.1.

Let's consider how payments are done in the financial system presented by Fig. 5.1. We have in mind the economics of payments in Freeman (1996). s means to complete an economic transaction by paying some kind of compensation. Freeman presents a model in which two types of securities, i.e., fiat money and IOU are endogenously valuable, and the former has payment function while the latter does not.

The public sector supplies two types of securities i.e., government bonds and the monetary base. Government bonds issued by the government do not have a payment function, but the monetary base supplied by the central bank has a payment function. On the other hand, demand deposits provided by financial institutions in the private sector also have a payment function. This is why it is said that "banks supply currency." In the following, we will reconsider the monetary base at the central bank accounts and the money stock (money supply) supplied by the financial institutions in the framework of the financial system.

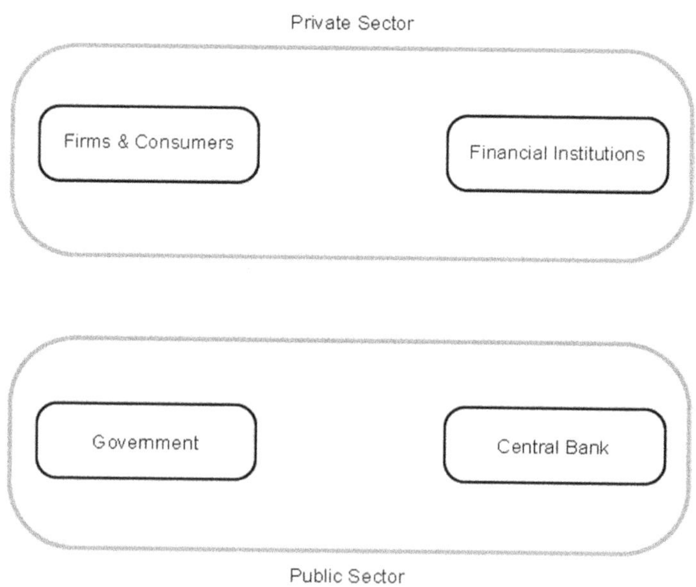

Fig. 5.1 Financial system: macroeconomic framework with financial institutions incorporated. *Note* While the government and the central bank separately administrate each policy in previous Fig. 3.4. Figure 5.1 has adopted an integrated style of fiscal and monetary policy. Consequently, as you will see the private sector takes economic activities in response to integrated fiscal and monetary policies

The monetary base is a currency supplied by the central bank and is defined as the sum of the circulating currency and the central bank's current accounts.The central bank as a supplier of the monetary base is at the position of a technical monopoly.[1] The monetary base is defined as follows.

$$\text{Monetary base} = \text{Currency in Circulation} + \text{Current Account Deposits in Central Bank}$$

where

$$\text{Currency in Circulation} = \text{Banknotes in Circulation} + \text{Coins in Circulation.}$$

On the other hand, the money stock is the currency supplied by financial institutions, and in a narrow sense, it is the sum of circulating currency and deposit currency.[2] The providers of deposit currency are the financial institutions. In addition, currency in circulation is added in the money stock. Therefore, the monetary base and the money stock are, by definition, moneys that contain currency in circulation in common, but both hold finality.[3] The money stock (M1) is defined as follows.

$$\text{M1} = \text{Currency in Circulation} + \text{Deposit Money Deposited at Depository Institutions}$$

By subtracting the circulating currency respectively from the definitions of the monetary base and the money stock, the current account deposit in the central bank and the deposit currency supplied by the financial institutions are specified. Two groups of currencies with finality are derived.

$$\text{Current Account Deposit in Central Bank} = \text{Monetary Base} - \text{Cash in Circulation}$$

$$\text{Deposit Currency in Financial Institutions} = \text{Money Stock} - \text{Cash in Circulation}$$

Figure 5.2 depicts how payments are made through these currencies in the presented financial system. It can be more clearly understood that the monetary base is the currency that processes interbank as well as the government payments as central bank current accounts, while most of the money stock is the currency supplied by financial institutions. The monetary base is a currency in which a central bank can decide on the supply of its quantity, and the portion of the money stock consisting of bank lending can be said to be a currency that is endogenously determined according to private demand for funds.

In addition to securities with finality, government checks and government bonds belonging to the class of IOUs will be incorporated into the trading mechanism.

---

[1] Milton Friedman (1953).

[2] In Japan, M1, M2, M3, and L (liquidity in a broad sense) are published as indices of the money stock. Here, we will proceed with the discussion with the narrow sense of M1 in mind. See Bank of Japan (2021).

[3] The debate over private cryptocurrencies will be ignored in these arguments.

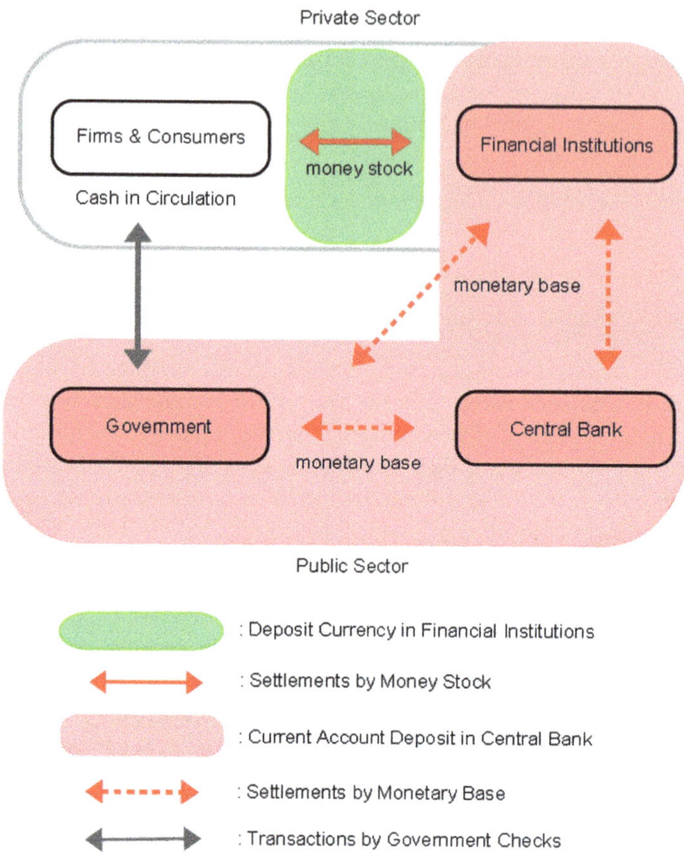

Fig. 5.2 Financial system from viewpoint of payment. *Note* This figure shows the current account deposit in central bank from the monetary base and deposit currency in financial institutions from the money stock and the payment part of each. In addition, the random matching model of Kiyotaki and Wright (1989) is positioned in the analysis of the "Cash in Circulation" part. The bank run problem of Diamond and Dybvig (1983) is an analysis of the "Firms & Consumers" and "Deposit Currency in Financial Institutions" parts

While the government pays with government checks when purchasing goods and services from private sector, it issues government bonds to finance it. Therefore, in this model, four securities contribute to transactions: the monetary base, the money stock, government checks, and government bonds.

How would transactions between the public sector and the private sector be conducted through financial institutions in this framework? The impact of fiscal expenditure i.e., transactions between the government and firms & consumers on prices will be analyzed.

5.2 Central Bank as Recipient of Government Bonds

We will show that fiscal policy can be a determinant of the price level in this financial system. The mechanism also satisfies the condition by Sims (2013) that fiscal policy and monetary policy are intertwined and tied together. Fiscal policy particularly draws the money stock from financial institutions by way of government checks. In addition, the claim by Kelton (2020), fiscal deficits increase our wealth and collective savings can be observed in this financial system. We present two types of FTPL mechanisms according to who is a recipient of government bonds both of which has the same result after all transactions. We will analyze the case in which the central bank purchases government bonds (public debt) and the case in which private financial institutions purchase them.

The first is the case in which the central bank is the recipient of government bonds. Under the assumption of S(TAB), let us consider the following sequence of transactions depicted in Fig. 5.3.[4] We fictitiously suppose this the case of the US.

Step 1. The government issues government checks to make public expenditure while firms and consumers receive them as a consideration for it.

Step 2. Firms and consumers get the money stock as deposit currency from the financial institutions through government checks.

Step 3. The financial institutions obtain the monetary base in exchange for government checks from the government.

Step 4. The government issues government bonds which are underwritten by the central bank to obtain the monetary base to pay government checks.[5]

In steps 1 and 2, fiscal spending directly drags out the money stock from the financial institutions. As a result, an increase in the money stock contributes to rising prices. This trading is guaranteed by the process of transferring the money base to be supplied by the central bank to financial institutions via government accounts in the step 4. Here, fiscal policy and monetary policy are inseparably linked to determine price level. Sims' assertion "fiscal policy can be the sole determinant of the price level in which monetary and fiscal policies mutually function" is satisfied.

In this process, the central bank has the function to provide unlimited central bank currency at any time. In other words, it has an ability to purchase government bonds indefinitely from the government and financial institutions. This means that in the step 3, when the financial institutions ask the government to buy government checks, it immediately requests the central bank to accept the government bonds to obtain the monetary base. Notice the government takes the activity of spending first and getting a source of revenues last according to S(TAB) i.e., spending precedes taxing

---

[4] Sims (2013) did not introduce S(TAB) in his arguments. This assumption is set here to be consistent with the MMT discussion described below.

[5] Assembling the process described in Fig. 5.3 in the order of Step 4, Step 1, Step 2, and Step 3, the structure of government spending is TAB(S). This is the behavior of households whose revenues are budgeted ahead of expenditure, as presented by Kelton (2020). Nevertheless, the reason for adopting S(TAB) here is that we assume central banks can underwrite government bonds indefinitely.

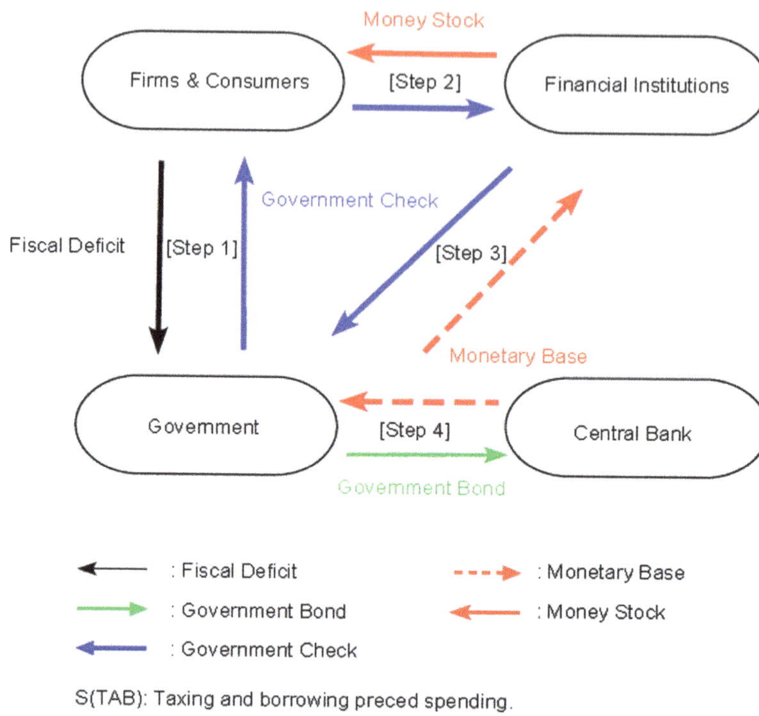

Fig. 5.3 Case of central bank as recipient of government bonds. *Note* Government spending causes an increase in the money stock by Step 2 while the monetary base functions to achieve this by steps 3 and 4. Fiscal policy is a determinant of the price level, and the monetary policy is in a position of support

and borrowing. On the other hand, the central bank is the final holder of government bonds in the step 4, which means a kind of monetization.

In a series of Quantitative and Qualitative Monetary Easing (QQE), inflation expectations were the driving force for price rise, and inflation targeting and forward guidance for the yield curve were the means to achieve this. The massive supply of the monetary base was hopefully expected to raise prices through an increase in the money stock. However, in the mechanism presented here fiscal spending artificially increases the money stock without relying on expectations, provided that the central bank underwrites government bonds. It appears only through tradings between the government and the central bank on a micro-foundation.

In addition, Kelton's Reality for Myth #4, i.e., "fiscal deficits increase our wealth and collective savings" can be derived in this financial system. Suppose we cancel out the trading process of government checks in Fig. 5.3, then we can only observe the relationship between the public sector and the private sector described in Fig. 5.4. Since government-issued loans are finally redeemed, as an ex-post phenomenon, transactions by government checks look disappeared in this mechanism. In Fig. 5.4, it is the situation claimed by the MMT proposition from the viewpoint of the model

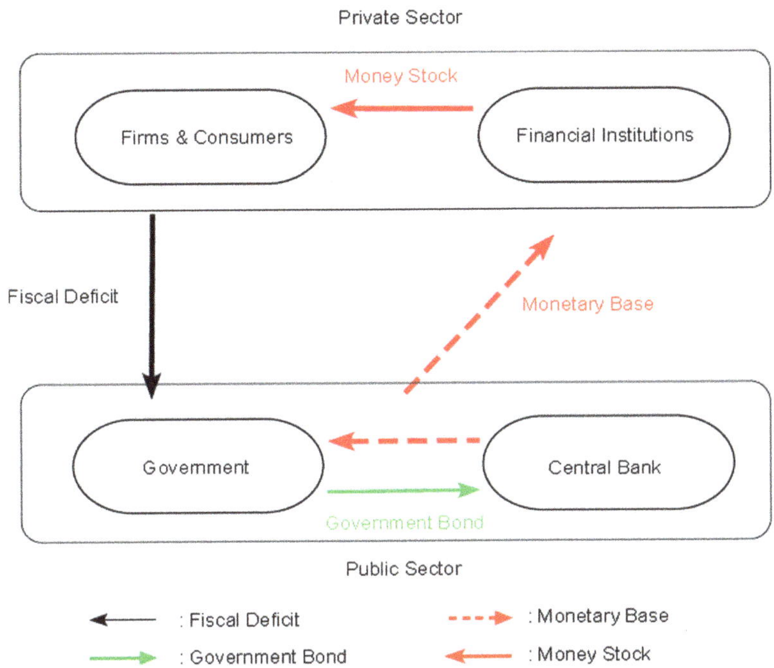

Fig. 5.4 Observation from viewpoint of MMT. *Note* The government's debt to cover fiscal expenditure (issuance of government bonds) is completed by the transfer of the monetary base to private financial institutions (an increase in deposits). It means government debt manifests itself in an increase in private savings

consisting of government and non-government sectors. Fiscal deficits as new issue of government bonds become our wealth and collective savings as the increase of the monetary base for the financial institutions. In other words, in the public sector, government debt is recorded as assets on the central bank's balance sheet, which is manifested as an increase in public debt as the increase of government bonds, while in the private sector, an increase in deposit currency (the money stock) occurs. This phenomenon is also true in the following case when the financial institutions directly purchase government bonds.

5.3 Financial Institutions as Recipient of Government Bonds

Here, we will consider the case where the financial institutions directly underwrite government bonds, which looks like the case of Japanese monetary market. The mechanism is comprised of 5 steps in 2 stages, i.e., steps 1–4 of first stage and step

5 of the second stage. Figure 5.5 describes the above series of transaction processes divided into stages 1 and 2.

1st stage consists of the following 4 steps.

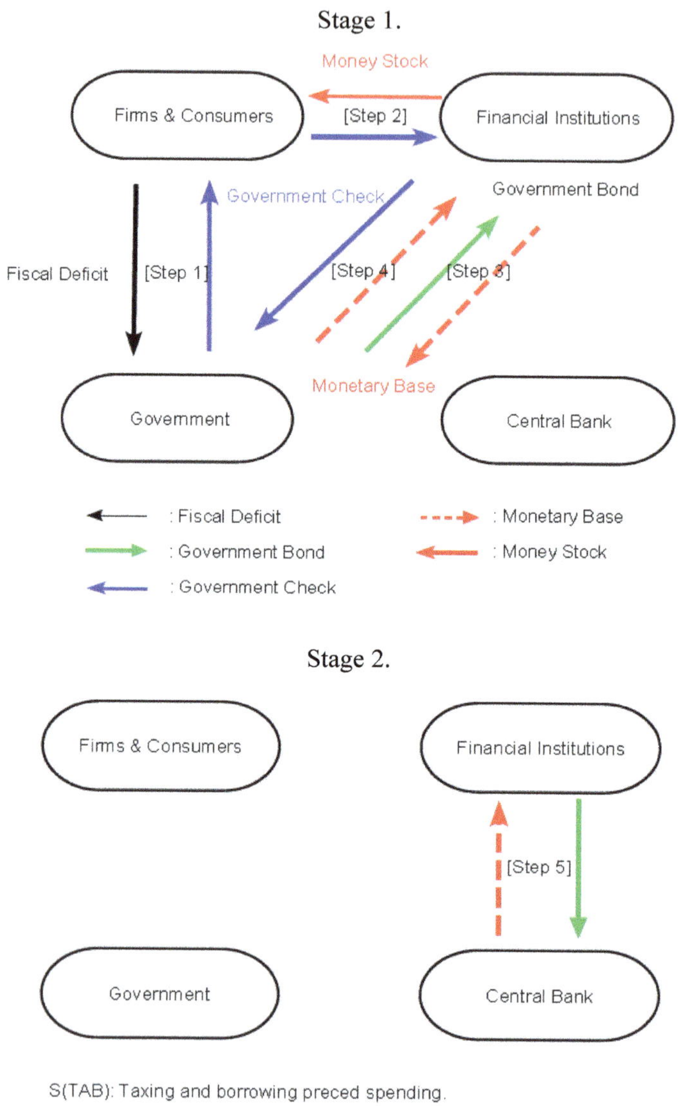

Fig. 5.5 Case of financial institutions as recipient of government bonds. *Note* In the stage 1, while fiscal spending causes an increase in the money stock, in this mechanism the purchaser of government bonds is a financial institution. The government issues and collects government checks. In the stage 2, the step 5 operations guarantee the sale of government bonds in the step 4

Step 1. The Government issues government checks to make public expenditure while firms and consumers receive them as payment.

Step 2. Firms and consumers get the money stock as deposit currency from the financial institutions by way of government checks.

Step 3. The government issues government bonds to obtain the monetary base from the financial institutions.

Step 4. The financial institutions obtain monetary base from the government in exchange for government checks.

Then 2nd stage is as follows.

Step 5. By the funds supplying operation, the central bank buys government bonds by paying the monetary base for the financial institutions.

The step 3 means the government sells government bonds to financial institutions in preparation for their requests to pay government checks. The government bonds are sold in the step 3 since they are guaranteed to be bought by the central bank in the step 5. Namely, the step 5 supports the step 3 for the government bonds to be sold out. The step 5 is necessary since government bonds must be valuable in the process of backward solution. Without the step 5, government bonds cannot be valuable. As in the previous case, it is assumed that the central bank as a permanent facility has the function to provide unlimited central bank currency at any time and purchase government bonds indefinitely from the government and financial institutions. Therefore, government behavior S(TAB) has been guaranteed.

Purchasing large amounts of government bonds in a series of QQEs corresponds to the step 5, which means supporting the price of the government bond market in the step 3. However, in Japan since fiscal spending has been restrained during this period, the money stock (bank lending) has not increased, and prices have not risen. Suppose except for the stage 1 which explains fiscal spending, only the stage 2 remains. Then, the money stock does not increase under the massive purchases of JGBs, only the monetary base held by the financial institutions increases. This is nothing but the monetary policy of Japan depicted in Fig. 3.4. It is the case in Japan we have so far worried about.

Now we will consider whether REALITY (MYTH 4) by Kelton (2020) can hold in this mechanism. Let's cancel out the processes of government checks and the monetary base in the stage 1. Then in Fig. 5.6 we can observe the relationship between the public sector and the private sector, i.e., the government deficit means non-government surplus.[6]

What are we able to get from the arguments so far?

(1) Whether the recipient of government bonds is a central bank or a financial institution, "fiscal policy can be the sole determinant of the price level" holds. In their mechanisms, fiscal policy directly pulls out the money stock by way of government checks while monetary policy provides the monetary base by

[6] In ex-post, the case of Sect. 5.3 is in the same situation as case of Sect. 5.2. Since MMT assumes that the monetary base and government bonds are identical, the proposition of MMT holds true even if the transfer of wealth from the government sector to the private sector is the monetary base or government bonds.

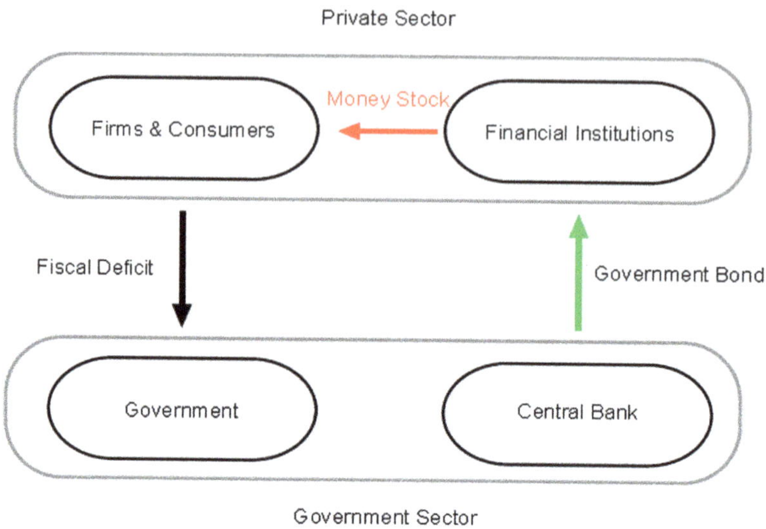

Fig. 5.6 Observation between public sector and private sector. *Note* Looking at the stage 1 from the perspectives of the government and non-government sectors, Kelton's (2020) proposition "Budget deficits are private wealth" emerges. Adding the stage 2 to the stage 1 and canceling out the transactions by government bonds transactions yields the result depicted in Fig. 5.4

operations. Notice fiscal policy cannot work without the role of the central bank. On the other hand, monetary policy alone merely increases the monetary base and does not affect the money stock. It means by Sims (2013) that "fiscal policy and monetary policy are intertwined and tied together." It is a well-known fact that fiscal spending is a policy tool for an economy to increase effective demand. In this discussion, we have shown that fiscal spending is a policy means of increasing the money stock in a macro model that incorporates financial institutions.

(2) In both mechanisms it is possible for the government to take the activity S(TAB) which is the main assumption of MMT since the central bank can unlimitedly provide central bank money (the monetary base), which means central bank can buy government bonds at will. As a result, FTPL and MMT are consistent as parts of a mechanism, and the assertion of MMT is shown as an ex-post phenomenon in Figs. 5.4 and 5.6. From the comparison of the two cases described, it is clear why MMT treats the monetary base and government bonds equally. In other words, MMT's assertion is supported by the assumption of homogeneity of the monetary base and government bonds, and currency supply right of the central bank.

References

Bank of Japan. Research and Statistic Department. Guide to Japan's Money Stock Statistics. May 2021.

Diamond. Douglas W. and Philip H. Dybvig. 1983. "Bank runs, deposit insurance, and liquidity," *Journal of Political Economy*, Vol. 91, 401–419.

Freeman, Scott. 1996. "The payment system, liquidity, and rediscounting, " American Economic Review, Vol. 86, 1126–38.

Friedman, 1953. *Essays in Positive Economics.* University of Chicago Press.

Kelton, Stephanie. The Deficit Myth Modern Monetary Theory and the Birth of the People's Economy, Public Affairs. 2020.

Kiyotaki, Nobuhiro and Randall Wright. 1989. "On money as a medium of exchange." *Journal of Political Economy*, Vol. 97, 927–54.

Sims, A. Christopher. 2013. Paper Money. American Economic Review.103(2): 563–584.

Chapter 6
Answer to Question 3: Crocodile Mouth Theory versus Blanchard Claim

Abstract We theoretically analyze how public debt affects the economy. There are two opposing ideas: the heavy public debt leads to fiscal collapse, or it contributes to economic efficiency. First, we derive the condition under which the current public debt can be redeemed by refinancing government bonds. This means that there is the limit to government bonds issued, and if they exceed the maximum, it will not be possible for the government to repay the current public debt. Therefore, the assertion that "accumulated public debt must be reduced as soon as possible" is applicable. On the other hand, in the same model, we show that if the current public debt can be repaid, namely refinancing succeeds, the economy with the larger public debt is more efficient according to Pareto criterion. This corresponds to Blanchard's assertion that public debt contributes to economic welfare, not costs. Thus, these two conflicting claims can be explained coherently by clarifying whether the current public debt satisfies the redeemable condition.

The above discussion has presented the financial system in which fiscal and monetary policy is inseparably linked, fiscal policy is the determinant of the price level, and the modern monetary theory (MMT) can inevitably hold. Now, let's look at how the budget deficits play a role in the financial system. If the relationship between public debt and fiscal collapse is not theoretically clear, the discussion thus far has merely presented the mechanism of the relationship between public debts and prices. A story to describe the current economic policy in Japan is not complete. The object is here to clarify the nature of the fiscal deficits through numerical models under the assumptions of the fiscal theory of the price level (FTPL) and MMT so far. How should we think about the fiscal deficits? We present a model consistent with contradictory claims about public debt.

Question 3. The widespread notion is "public debt levels are too high and must urgently be decreased." Is public debt itself bad?

There are two opposing views on public debt. In Japan most of the arguments are that government debt levels are too high and must urgently be decreased, otherwise the economy will sooner or later lead to financial collapse. Public debt, which is the

Y. Sakai, *Deflation and Fiscal Deficits*, SpringerBriefs in Economics,
https://doi.org/10.1007/978-981-97-0415-6_6

difference between expenditure and revenue, is called as the crocodile mouth, and it has expanded over time. Japan's urgent economic task is to close the mouth of this crocodile. Let us call it the crocodile mouth theory. In contrast, Blanchard (2019) claims "public debt may have no fiscal cost" and "the welfare costs of public debt may be smaller than typically assumed" on page 1197. Blanchard even says "the model surely overstates the degree of non-Ricardian equivalence: debt in this economy is (nearly fully) net wealth" on page 1212. Blanchard analyzes economic welfare through comparative statics, but the following analyzes the competitive equilibrium from the perspective of different time points. Therefore, the analysis from now on theoretically compensates for Blanchard's open problem.

The crocodile mouth theory belongs to the Ricardian type of government while the Blanchard assertion and MMT argument are subject to non-Ricardian type of government. Would the crocodile mouth theory derived from the Japan situation and Blanchard's argument based on the U.S. economy theoretically be opposing ideas? Our analysis will suggest that these propositions are not necessarily at odds with each other but rather have common structure and may be consistently explained.

6.1 Model

Based on our argument so far, we will show a model in which the crocodile mouth theory and Blanchard's claim are compatible as the answer to the question 3. First, how much will the model here be able to fit the assumptions of FTPL and MMT? Before doing so, we will clarify the following two points in advance. Blanchard discusses public debt on the condition that the growth rate is above interest rates, but we do not consider this condition because the model is not involved with production technology. Second, the model is written in real terms because we will ask for a condition of redeemable public debt by indicating the existence of financial collapse. The reason for writing the model in real terms is to present an environment that describes both the situation where public debt increases efficiency and the situation of fiscal collapse, as explained below.

We construct the financial system comprised of government sector and non-government sector under Samuelson's pure consumption loan model as credit money i.e., fiat money trustworthy by the government instead of commodity money. We set up the identity of government bonds and the central bank money because of the assumption the central bank can unlimitedly buy the government bonds with the monetary base.

We start describing the government behavior, constructing the government budget constraint. Let G_t, T_t and B_t be respectively the public expenditure, tax revenue and the government bonds at period t. The government budget constraint is described as

$$G_t + B_{t-1} = T_t + B_t/r_t.$$

The left side is the sum of government expenditures and redemption government bonds, and the right side is revenue consisting of tax revenues and newly issued government bonds.

The government borrows from the young, issuing one-period bonds. Suppose that the government issues B_t units of bonds in period t, it will need to pay these bonds off in period $t + 1$ with B_t units of the time $t + 1$ good. The government bonds are backed money since the government promised to pay at time $t + 1$ 1 unit of the time $t + 1$ good for each of the bonds that the government sold at time t.[1] Let r_t be the gross real interest rate at period t, which is measured in terms of the time $t + 1$ good per unit of the time t good.[2] Owing to the one-period bonds, the government can choose each period to pay off the previous issued loans by issuing new ones, i.e., debt rollovers which is formulated as

$$\forall t \geq 1 : B_{t+1} = r_{t+1} B_t$$

which is an assumption of the government behavior in both Sims (2013) and Blanchard (2019). The debt rollover condition implies not only the policy behavior of the government but also the function of the central bank under the equivalence of the monetary base and the government bonds in this setup.

Define D_t the fiscal deficit at time t as.

$$D_t \overset{def}{\equiv} G_t - T_t.$$

Then the government budget constraint turns out

$$D_t = B_t / r_t - B_{t-1} \tag{6.1}$$

This budget constraint incorporates the fiscal backup by the assumptions: the function of central banks as permanent facility of the monetary base provision and the homogeneity of government bonds and the monetary base. Then, the government policy at time $t \geq 1$ is represented by the sequence $\{D_t, B_t\}_{t=1}^{\infty}$, subject to the rule of debt rollovers and the government budget constraint.[3]

We specify the sequence of the government deficits $\{D_t\}_{t=1}^{\infty}$ as

$$D_1 > 0 \text{ and } D_t = 0 \text{ for } t \geq 2. \tag{6.2}$$

Equation (6.2) describes that the government first makes decision of expenditure D_1 as for example the funds for the social security, which are distributed equally the old at time 1. After that, the government chooses each period to pay off old loans by issuing new loan by debt rollovers. So, the first period fiscal deficits by the

---

1 The unit of display of the government bonds B_t is written by the notation $[t + 1\text{good}]$.

2 The unit of display of r_t is represented by the notation, [time $t + 1$ good / time t good].

3 We assume $B_0 = 0$.

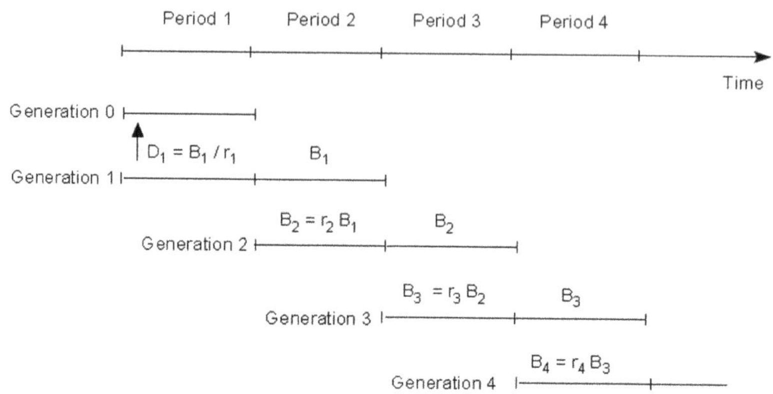

Fig. 6.1 Government behavior subject to S(TAB) and Debt Rollovers. *Note* In the first period, the government first determines the public debt D_1 in accordance with S(TAB), and covers it by issuing government bonds B_1. The government then pays off the public debt according to the debt rollovers i.e., $B_{t+1} = r_{t+1}B_t$ for $t \geq 1$. In addition, the model does not distinguish between government bonds and the monetary base by the assumption of MMT

government, D_1 is the sole determinant as a policy choice. Notice that government takes activity S(TAB) under debt rollover See Fig. 6.1.

One of the conveniences on the assumption of the first period deficit only and one period bonds is that when we consider the future deficit $D_k > 0$ for $k > 1$ as an additional expenditure, we can take the fiscal deficit at period k as the new starting period, adding newly issued bonds. We will see this benefit in the proof of proposition 4.

As to the private market, we describe the two-period-lived consumer behavior. The population of generation t is defined by N_t for $t \geq 0$. Let n be the growth rate of population.

$$N_{t+1} = nN_t \text{ for } t \geq 0.$$

Let c_{1t}^h and $c_{2,t+1}^h$ be respectively the consumptions of young and old for a member $h \in N_t$. Similarly, w_{1t}^h and $w_{2,t+1}^h$ are the initial endowments of young and of old for a member $h \in N_t$.[4] The current old ($t = 1$) only care about their current consumption c_{21}^h while both current and future young have the preferences represented by the utility function $u_t^h(c_{1t}^h, c_{2,t+1}^h)$. Let ℓ_t^h be the private loans (the lending or the borrowing) of the member $h \in N_t$ for $t \geq 1$. Let b_t^h and p_t^b be respectively the holdings of government bonds for a member of a member $h \in N_t$ of generation t, and the price of government bonds in period t. In particular, p_t^b is measured as the price of time $t + 1$ good in terms of time t good.

A young consumers problem is

[4] Since the economy starts at $t = 1$, c_{10}^h and w_{10}^h do not exist or cannot be defined. Only c_{21}^h and w_{21}^h are meaningful at $t = 1$.

$$\max_{c^h_{1t}, c^h_{2,t+1}} u^h_t\left(c^h_{1t}, c^h_{2,t+1}\right)$$

s.t.

$$c^h_{1t} = w^h_{1t} - \ell^h_t - p^b_t b^h_t \tag{6.3}$$

when young, and

$$c^h_{2,t+1} = w^h_{2,t+1} + r_t \ell^h_t + b^h_t \tag{6.4}$$

when old.

Combining these budget constraints (6.3) and (6.4) by substituting out ℓ^h_t gives

$$c^h_{1t} + c^h_{2,1+t}/r_t = w^h_{1t} + w^h_{2,t+1}/r_t - b^h_t\left(p^b_t - 1/r_t\right). \tag{6.5}$$

By (6.5) we get the condition that the rate of return on government bonds is equal to the return on private borrowing and lending is called the arbitrage condition,[5]

$$r_t = 1/p^b_t. \tag{6.6}$$

6.2 Temporary Equilibrium and Sequential Pareto Criteria

We will analyze the inter-temporal economy according to Pareto criterion. We define the temporary equilibrium as the sequence of the competitive equilibrium at any time $t \geq 1$. The competitive equilibrium for $\forall t \geq 1$ is defined by (i) utility maximization and (ii) the market clearing condition The young maximize their utility subject to the budget constraints and derive individually the savings function $s^h_t(r_t)$. On the other hand, the current old ($t = 1$) will maximize only their current consumption, c^h_{21}.

The model has two monetary assets i.e., private loans and the government bonds. By the arbitrage condition (6), the common rate of returns of both assets is r_t. Since we assume that each member of each generation is identical, the aggregate amounts of the private loans are zero. Therefore, the government bonds play a role of the store of value and the debt rollovers of government bonds play a role of the linkage between the sequential temporary equilibrium. Let S_t be the aggregate savings function (total sum of each individual savings function $s^h_t(r_t)$), which is the function of r_t. The utility maximization for the young and the market clearing condition are described by the equation,

$$S_t(r_t) = B_t/r_t \text{ for } t \geq 1 \tag{6.7}$$

[5] Without the arbitrage condition, the equilibrium with two monetary assets valued does not hold.

where

$$S_t(r_t) = \sum_{h=1}^{N_t} s_t^h(r_t) \text{ and } B_t = \sum_{h=1}^{N_t} b_t^h.$$

Then, suppose that a sequence of policy set $\{D_t\}_{t=1}^{\infty}$ is given, the temporary equilibrium is described as the sequence $\{c_{2t}^h, c_{1t}^h, b_t^h \text{ for } h \in N_{t-1}, r_t\}_{t=1}^{\infty}$.

Definition 1 (*temporary equilibrium*). Given a sequence of policy set $\{D_t\}_{t=1}^{\infty}$, a temporary equilibrium is the sequence of time t competitive equilibrium $\{c_{2t}^h, c_{1t}^h, b_t^h \text{ for } h \in N_{t-1}, r_t\}_{t=1}^{\infty}$ such that the equilibrium conditions.

(i) $D_1 = B_1/r_1$ (initial condition),
(ii) $B_{t+1} = r_{t+1}B_t$ (debt rollovers),
(iii) $S_t^b(r_t) = B_t/r_t$ (market clearing condition) are fulfilled.

According to the sequence of the deficits by (2), given D_1 the temporary equilibrium is described by the sequence of competitive equilibrium. Let $\{B_t(D_1)\}_t^{\infty}$ be the sequence of the government bonds in the temporary equilibrium when the financial deficit D_1 as a policy parameter is given. We call the path of government bonds redeemable when $\{B_t(D_1)\}_t^{\infty}$ converges to zero,

$$\lim_{t\to\infty} B_t(D_1) = 0.$$

Now, we have a sequence $\{B_t(D_1)\}_{t=1}^{\infty}$ describing a redeemable path of government bonds in the inter-temporal economy. From now on, we will seek the sufficient condition of D_1 supporting the redeemable path of the government bonds. In addition, we need Pareto criteria to evaluate the sequence of temporary equilibrium.

Let C_t and Y_t be respectively the total consumption and the total endowments defined as

$$C_t \overset{def}{\equiv} \sum_{h=1}^{N_{t-1}} c_{2t}^h + \sum_{h=1}^{N_{t-1}} c_{1t}^h \text{ for } \forall t \geq 1$$

and

$$Y_t \overset{\text{def}}{=} \sum_{h=1}^{N_{t-1}} w_{2t}^h + \sum_{h=1}^{N_t} w_{1t}^h \text{ for } \forall t \geq 1.$$

The feasibility condition is defined as follows.

Definition 2 (*feasibility*). A sequence of consumption allocations $\{c_{21}^h \text{ for } h \in N_0, (c_{1t}^h, c_{2t}^h)) \text{ for } h \in N_t\}_{t=1}^{\infty}$ is feasible if

$$C_t \leq Y_t \quad \text{for } \forall t \geq 1.$$

is satisfied.

In the inter-temporal economy, the consumption allocation is described by the sequence $\{c_{21}^h \text{ for } h \in N_0, (c_{1t}^h, c_{2t}^h) \text{ for } h \in N_t\}_{t=1}^{\infty}$. Then the sequence of preferences is given as $\{c_{21}^h \text{ for } h \in N_0, u_t^h(c_{1t}^h, c_{2t}^h) \text{ for } h \in N_t\}_{t=1}^{\infty}$. Sequential Pareto criteria as the instrument to evaluate the sequence of temporary equilibrium are introduced by,

Definition 3 (*sequential Pareto optimality*).

(i) Consider two feasible sequences of individual consumptions, $\{\hat{c}_{21}^h \text{ for } h \in N_0, (\hat{c}_{1t}^h, \hat{c}_{2t}^h) \text{ for } h \in N_t\}_{t=1}^{\infty}$ and $\{c_{21}^h \text{ for } h \in N_0, (c_{1t}^h, c_{2t}^h) \text{ for } h \in N_t\}_{t=1}^{\infty}$. The former is sequential Pareto superior to the latter, when at least one strict inequality holds in the following set of inequalities,

$$c_{21}^h \leq \hat{c}_{21}^h \text{ for } \forall h \in N_0$$

and

$$u_t^h(c_{1t}^h, c_{2,t+1}^h) \leq u_t^h(\hat{c}_{1t}^h, \hat{c}_{2,t+1}^h) \text{ for} \forall h \in N_t, \forall t \geq 1.$$

(ii) A feasible sequence is sequential Pareto optimal if there does not exist any feasible sequence that is sequential Pareto superior to it.

6.3 Do Fiscal Deficits Burden Economic Welfare?

Here, giving the model Cobb–Douglas utility function we will derive the sufficient condition of the redeemable sequence of government bonds. The reason of the specification is to obtain clear claims from viewpoint of the macro-economic framework despite loss of generalization. It is easy to get the same results in other utility function. Proofs of the following propositions are given in Appendix.

The population, preferences and the initial endowments are specified as

$$N_t = 100 \text{ for } t \geq 0,$$

$$u_t^h = c_{1t}^h c_{2,t+1}^h \quad \text{for } t \geq 1,$$

$$(w_{1t}^h, w_{2t}^h) = (2, 1) \quad \text{for } t \geq 1.$$

Namely, the population is constant, $\forall t \geq 0 : N_{t+1} = nN_t$, i.e. the growth rate of population $(n = 1)$ and the initial endowments are much weighted in the youth rather than in the old.[6] We seek the sequence of the redeemable government bonds in the temporary equilibrium given the initial transfer D_1 from the young to the old.

Proposition 1 (the redeemability of fiscal deficit).

(i) $\forall D_1 (0 < D_1 < 50) : \lim_{t \to \infty} B_t(D_1) = 0$.
(ii) $\forall t \geq 1 : B_t(0) = 0$.
(iii) $\forall t \geq 1 : B_t(50) = 50$.

Proposition 1 is the sufficient condition with respect to the initial fiscal deficit D_1 whether the sequence of the government bonds $\{B_t(D_1)\}_{t=1}^{\infty}$ is redeemable. If the outstanding debt given as an initial condition is within the threshold, under the debt rollovers the redeemable route of redemption will be taken. On the other hand, if the outstanding debt deviates from the threshold, it will lead to financial collapse. This is the claim of the crocodile mouth theory. Therefore, it became clear that under the debt rollovers, the process is divided according to the outstanding debt. How economic welfare will evolve when the outstanding amount of government bonds issued is in the process of convergence will be discussed below.

Another endogenous variable determined in the temporary equilibrium is the gross rate of return of which sequence $\{r_t(D_1)\}_{t=1}^{\infty}$ has the following properties where $r_t(D_1)$ is the gross interest rate at period t given the initial fiscal deficits, D_1.

Proposition 2 (the effect of fiscal deficit on interest rates).

(i) $\forall D_1 (0 < D_1 < 50) : \lim_{t \to \infty} r_t(D_1) = 1/2$
(ii) $\forall t \geq 1 : r_t(0) = 1/2$, and $\forall t \geq 1 : r_t(50) = 1$
(iii) If $D_1 < D_1' (0 < D_1 < D_1' < 50)$, *then* $\forall t \geq 1 : r_t(D_1) < r_t'(D_1')$.

We comment the difference of the setting from Blanchard (2019) including capital accumulation which argues on the costs of public debt when safe interest rates are low. The main proposition of Blanchard is if the interest rate is less than the growth rate, then the transfer is welfare improving. In contrast, we show that if $\forall D_1 \in (0, 50)$, then $\forall t \geq 1 : 1/2 < r_t(D_1) < 1$, and $\{r_t(D_1)\}_{t=1}^{\infty}$ is monotonically decreasing in proof of Proposition 2. The sequence of interest rates satisfies the condition of low interest rates by Blanchard. It is consistent with the situation of Blanchard.

Proposition 2 (iii) has a meaning, which says that the increment of the fiscal deficit makes the interest rate rise. By way of the arbitrage condition (6) it implies a linkage between the fiscal deficit and the price of monetary asset, the government bonds since p_t^b is the price of time $t + 1$ good in terms of time t good. The increment of the fiscal deficit implies that the price of the government bonds is going down.[7] The fiscal parameter can affect the price of monetary asset, the government bonds.[8] We will use the Propositions 1 and 2 when we analyze the economic welfare.

---

[6] One of the reasons we adopt the specific utility function is that we will analyze the inter-temporal approach to evaluate the sequence of temporary equilibrium.

[7] $D_1' < D_1' (0 < D_1' < D_1' < 50) \Rightarrow \forall t \geq 1 : r_t < r_t' \Rightarrow \forall t \geq 1 : p_t^{b'} < p_t^b$.

[8] Sims (2013) says that in the literature on FTPL the fiscal policy can be a determinant, or even the sole determinant, of the price level. This model is the first step although it surely does not cover whole story of FTPL.

From Propositions 1 and 2, we have three patterns of the paths of redeemable government bonds $\{B_t\}_{t=1}^{\infty}$ according to the fiscal deficit at the first period, $D_1 \in [0, 50]$. Let $\mathrm{Eq^m}\ \{B_t(0)\}_{t=1}^{\infty}$, $\mathrm{Eq^m}\ \{B_t(D_1)\}_{t=1}^{\infty}$ and $\mathrm{Eq^m}\ \{B_t(50)\}_{t=1}^{\infty}$ be respectively such sequences when the fiscal deficit, $D_1 = 0$, $0 < D_1 < 50$ or $D_1 = 50$ is given. We call $\mathrm{Eq^m}\ \{B_t(0)\}_{t=1}^{\infty}$ status quo (nothing change), $\mathrm{Eq^m}\ \{B_t(D_1)\}_{t=1}^{\infty}$ $(0 < D_1 < 50)$ the redeemable path, and $\mathrm{Eq^m}\ \{B_t(50)\}_{t=1}^{\infty}$ steady state. Then we will evaluate each sequence of temporary equilibrium according to sequential Pareto criteria introduced above.

Proposition 3 (the welfare analysis of the fiscal deficit).

(i) $\mathrm{Eq^m}\ \{B_t(D_1)\}_{t=1}^{\infty}$ $(0 < D_1 < 50)$ is sequential Pareto superior to $\mathrm{Eq^m}\ \{B_t(0)\}_{t=1}^{\infty}$.
(ii) $\mathrm{Eq^m}\ \left\{B_t(50)\right\}_{t=1}^{\infty}$ is sequential Pareto superior to any $\mathrm{Eq^m}\ \left\{B_t\left(D_1\right)\right\}_{t=1}^{\infty}$ where $0 < D_1 < 50$.
(iii) $\mathrm{Eq^m}\ \{B_t(50)\}_{t=1}^{\infty}$ is sequential Pareto optimal.
(iv) $\forall D_1, D_1' (0 < D_1 < D_1' < 50)$: $\mathrm{Eq^m}\ \left\{B_t\left(D_1'\right)\right\}_{t=1}^{\infty}$ is sequential Pareto superior to $\mathrm{Eq^m}\ \{B_t(D_1)\}_{t=1}^{\infty}$
(v) $\forall D_1 \in (0, 50)$ and $t < t'$: $\mathrm{Eq^m}\ B_t(D_1)$ is sequential Pareto superior to $\mathrm{Eq^m}\ B_{t'}\left(D_1\right)$.[9]

The economic implication of proposition 3 are as follows. Proposition 3 (i) means any temporary equilibrium under the redeemable path of the government bonds is sequential Pareto superior to the status quo, the case of no fiscal deficit. This means that the issuance of government bonds (government debt) is not itself evil. Proposition 3 (ii) and (iii) suggest that there exists a sequence of government bonds leading to the optimal outstanding amount of government bonds.

As to proposition 3 (iv), suppose that we consider two fiscal deficits D_1 and D_1' $(D_1 < D_1')$ both of which are on the redeemable path. Then, for any $t \geq 1$ the temporary equilibrium with the fiscal deficit D_1' is sequential Pareto superior to the temporary equilibrium with the government deficits D_1. It turns out whenever a fiscal deficit is redeemable, the heavier fiscal deficit is preferable. Therefore, proposition 3 (iv) is a situation where Blanchard's assertion "public debt is net wealth" applies. This result is against the widespread notion of the crocodile mouth theory because we have usually thought that the heavy fiscal deficits give the bad effects to the economy. Namely the usual opinion (Ricardian equivalence) is that the fiscal deficits issuing extra government bonds will cause the future taxes for the redemption of it and lead to the bad expectations for the future economy.

On the other hand, proposition (v) is a comparison among each competitive equilibrium in the process of temporary equilibrium that follows an identical process. Under the redeemable path of the government bonds, a temporary equilibrium at time t is Pareto superior to a temporary equilibrium at future time t', where $t < t'$.It means that people in the process of the redeemable government bonds have always suffered the current economic situation because they feel the economic welfare deteriorating.

[9] $\mathrm{Eq}^m\ B_t(D_1)$ is defined as the competitive equilibrium at period t as an element of the sequence of the temporary equilibrium.

To sum up, the model describes situations in which the crocodile mouth theory applies in proposition 1 by the existence of a financial collapse, while proposition 3 (iv) derives Blanchard's assertion in case satisfying the redeemable condition. Proposition 3 (iv) and (v) are meaningful from the viewpoint of the political operation. It suggests that the government tends to repeat issuing new government bonds if the fiscal deficits satisfy the redeemable condition.[10] We will clarify this finding in the following.

6.4 Why Does Public Debt Continue to Rise Despite the Huge Budget Deficit?

We have so far analyzed the fiscal deficit at the first period D_1 as a sole determinant of the motion of the economy and evaluated the sequence of temporary equilibria. Here we will consider the case of the additional deficit at period $k > 1$ in the middle of the redeemable process. Let $D_k > 0$ be the deficit additionally imposed by the government at period k. The sequence of the fiscal deficit $\{D_t\}_{t=1}^{\infty}$ is described as

$$\{D_t\}_{t=1}^{\infty} = \{D_1, 0, \cdots, 0, D_k, 0, \cdots\}.$$

Let the sequence of the government bonds subject to this financial policy be

$$\left\{B_t\left(D_1, D_k\right)\right\}_{t=1}^{\infty},$$

which can be represented as

$$\{B_t(D_1, D_k)\}_{t=1}^{\infty} = \begin{cases} \{B_t(D_1)\}_{t=1}^{k-1} \\ \\ \{B_t(D_1, D_k)\}_{t=k}^{\infty} \end{cases}$$

Take look at the period k in the sequence of temporary equilibrium, then

$$B_{k-1}(D_1) + D_k = B_k(D_1, D_k)/r_t \tag{6.8}$$

holds. The new fiscal deficit is the sum of the liquidation of the redeemable process of government bonds '$\{B_t(D_1)\}_{t=1}^{\infty}$ and the additional deficit D_k. The government issues the bond that promises to pay the amount of the consumption good at the period $k+1$, $B_k(D_1, D_k)$. So, (6.8) is the government budget constraint at the period k.

Taking period $k > 1$ as the new starting point, we also assume that by lemma 1 of proposition 1 in appendix the redeemable condition of the sequence of the government bonds at period k is

[10] We will show this idea as the exact statement in the following discussions.

$$0 < B_k(D_1, D_k) < 50.$$

Then the sequence $\{B_k(D_1, D_k)\}_{t=k}^{\infty}$ is redeemable. Now, let us compare two sequences, i.e., the original path without any additional fiscal deficit and the one with the additional fiscal deficit at period k. It is easily shown that the new path created by the additional fiscal deficit is sequential Pareto Superior to the original path.

Proposition 4 *Consider two sequences of fiscal policy,* $\{D_t\}_{t=1}^{\infty} = \{D_1, 0, \cdots\}$ *and* $\{D_t\}_{t=1}^{\infty} = \{D_1, 0, \cdots, 0, D_k, 0, \cdots\}$ *both of which satisfy the redeemable condition. The latter allocation is sequential Pareto superior to the former allocation.*

Proposition 4 means that by the newly issued government bonds in the process of redeemable path the government can make the economy move to sequential Pareto superior allocation. Therefore, the government repeatedly makes ready to issue the new government bonds in the middle of the fiscal reconstruction rather than to redeem the fiscal deficits completely.

Appendix

Proposition 1 (the redeemability of fiscal deficit).
(i) $\forall D_1 (0 < D_1 < 50) : \lim_{t\to\infty} B_t(D_1) = 0.$
(ii) $\forall t \geq 1 : B_t(0) = 0.$
(iii) $\forall t \geq 1 : B_t(50) = 50.$

Proof We proceed to make our arguments according to the following steps to obtain the sequence of the redeemable government bonds, given the initial fiscal deficit D_1.

Step 1. The government will find the sufficient condition of public debt B_1 in which the sequence $\{B_t\}_{t=1}^{\infty}$ is redeemable.[11]

Step 2. The government chooses the fiscal deficit D_1 which satisfies the redeemable condition of $\{B_t(D_1)\}_{t=1}^{\infty}$.

Now, we will show the relationship between the redeemable path of the government bonds and the initial fiscal deficit D_1. Before that, we will prove a couple of lemmas. In particular, lemma 1 and its corollary we describe the movements of the path of the government bonds $\{B_t\}_{t=1}^{\infty}$ according to the sufficient conditions of initial government bonds B_1. Lemma 2 and its corollary tell the relationship between B_1 and the fiscal deficit at the first period D_1 as a policy parameter of the government.

Lemma 1 (the redeemable condition on the government bonds).

$$\forall B_1 \in (0, 50) : \lim_{t\to\infty} B_t = 0$$

[11] We take the utility of the current old as $u_0^h = c_{21}^h$ for $h \in N_0$.

Proof Let us consider as the temporary equilibrium the sequence of the government bonds, $\{B_t\}_{t=1}^{\infty}$ when B_1 is given. First, we will show that the sequence $\{B_t\}_{t=1}^{\infty}$ is monotonically decreasing if $0 < B_1 < 50$. From Cobb–Douglas utility function, by the temporary equilibrium condition (iii) we have the aggregate savings function,

$$S_t(r_t) = 100(1 - 1/2r_t) = B_t/r_t.$$

Solving this equation for r_t, we have

$$r_t = B_t/100 + 1/2. \tag{A-1}$$

Substituting r_t into the deficit rollovers (definition 1 (ii)), we have the law which the sequence $\{B_t\}_{t=1}^{\infty}$ follows.

$$B_{t+1} = 50B_t/(100 - B_t) \text{ for t} \geq 1. \tag{A-2}$$

Let us verify the convergence of the sequence $\{B_t\}_{t=1}^{\infty}$. Take the difference between B_{t+1} and B_t.

$$B_{t+1} - B_t = 50B_t/(100 - B_t) - 50B_{t-1}/(100 - B_{t-1})$$

$$= 5000(B_t - B_{t-1})/(100 - B_t)(100 - B_{t-1}).$$

If $0 \leq B_t < 100(t \geq 1)$, $B_{t+1} - B_t$ and $B_t - B_{t-1}$ have the same sign. Now, take look at the condition $t = 1$ in (A-2),

$$B_2 - B_1 = 50B_1/(100 - B_1) - B_1 = \{(B_1 - 50)/(100 - B_1)\}B_1$$

If $0 < B_1 < 50$, $B_1 > B_2$ holds. Since $B_{t+1} - B_t$ and $B_t - B_{t-1}$ have the same sign, then.

$$B_1 > B_2 > B_3 > \ldots$$

holds. The sequence $\{B_t\}_{t=1}^{\infty}$ is monotonically decreasing. Therefore, we have found that $0 < B_1 < 50$ is the sufficient condition in which the sequence $\{B_t\}_{t=1}^{\infty}$ is monotonically decreasing.

Second, we will show that the sequence $\forall B_1 \in (0, 50) : \{B_t\}_{t=1}^{\infty}$ is bounded. Suppose that $0 < B_1 < 50$ when $t = 1$,

$$0 < 50B_1 < 2500 \text{ and}$$

$$50 < 100 - B_1 < 100$$

hold. By (A-2), we have

$$0 < B_2 = 50B_1/(100 - B_1) < 50$$

When $t = k \geq 2$, suppose

$$0 < B_k < 50$$

holds. Then, similarly by (A-2),

$$0 < B_{k+1} = 50B_k/(100 - B_k) < 50$$

holds. From the mathematical induction it follows that we have

$$\forall t \geq 1 : 0 < B_t < 50.$$

It means that $\{B_t\}_{t=1}^{\infty}$ is bounded. By convergence of the theorem of bounded monotonic sequence, when $0 < B_1 < 50$, the sequence of temporary equilibrium $\{B_t\}_{t=1}^{\infty}$ converges.

Finally, we will show that $\lim_{t\to\infty} B_t = 0$. Suppose that $\lim_{t\to\infty} B_t = B > 0$. By (A-2), we have

$$B = 50B/(100 - B)$$

which means that $B = 0$ or 50. Since $\{B_t\}_{t=1}^{\infty}$ is monotone decreasing when $0 < B_1 < 50$, we have $\lim_{t\to\infty} B_t = 0$. ■

We obtain the sufficient condition of a redeemable path of government bonds $\{B_t\}_{t=1}^{\infty}$ with respect to B_1, which is derived from the economic environments. We have immediately had the following corollary.

Corollary 1 (i) *When* $B_1 = 0, \forall t \geq 1 : B_t = 0$.
(ii) *When* $B_1 = 50, \forall t \geq 1 : B_t = 50$.

Proof (i) Taking $B_1 = 0$ in (A-2), we have $\forall t \geq 1 : B_t = 0$. ■

Proof (ii) Taking $B_1 = 50$ in (A-2), we have $\forall t \geq 1 : B_t = 50$. ■

We have found the sufficient condition on B_1 in which the sequence of the government bonds $\{B_t\}_{t=1}^{\infty}$ converges to zero. However, this is not the condition on D_1 that is a policy parameter. B_1 is derived from the economic environment while D_1 is decided by the government. Therefore, we need the following lemma that is linked between B_1 and D_1.

Lemma 2 (the relationship between public debt B_1 and fiscal deficit D_1). *The condition of redeemable path of the government bonds* ($0 < B_1 < 50$) *is equivalent to the condition of redeemable path of the fiscal deficit* ($0 < D_1 < 50$).

Proof ($\Rightarrow$) Start from the condition of the government bonds, $0 < B_1 < 50$. By the temporary equilibrium condition (iii) in period $t = 1$,

$$S_1(r_1) = 100(1 - 1/2r_1) = B_1/r_1$$

holds. Solve this equation for r_1,

$$r_1 = B_1/100 + 1/2$$

Substitute r_1 into the temporary equilibrium condition (i) and solve for B_1, we have.

$$B_1 = (1/2)\{100D_1/(100 - D_1)\}. \tag{A-3}$$

Since the condition of the redeemable path of the government bonds is $0 < B_1 < 50$, we have

$$0 < B_1 = (1/2)\{100D_1/(100 - D_1)\} < 50.$$

From l.h.s. of this equation,

$$0 < (1/2)\{100D_1/(100 - D_1)\}$$

we have $0 < D_1$. Similarly, from r.h.s. of this equation,

$$(1/2)\{100D_1/(100 - D_1)\} < 50$$

we have $D_1 < 50$. So, $0 < D_1 < 50$ holds.

($\Leftarrow$) Conversely, start from the condition of the fiscal deficit, $0 < D_1 < 50$. We have $0 < B_1 < 50$, vice versa. ■

By lemma 2, given D_1, the sequence of the government bonds, $\{B_t\}_{t=1}^{\infty}$ has the following properties.

Corollary 2 (i) $\forall t \geq 1 : B_t(0) = 0$.
(ii) $\forall t \geq 1 : B_t(50) = 50$.

Proof By (A-3), it is obvious to get the results. ■

By lemmas 1 and 2, proposition 1 is proved. ■

Proposition 2 (the effect of fiscal deficit on interest rates)
Let $r_t(D_1)$ be the gross interest rate given D_1.
(i) $\forall D_1 (0 < D_1 < 50) : \lim_{t\to\infty} r_t(D_1) = 1/2$.

(ii) $\forall t \geq 1 : r_t(0) = 1/2$, and $\forall t \geq 1 : r_t(50) = 1$.
(iii) If $D_1 < D_1' (0 < D_1 < D_1' < 50)$, then$\forall t \geq 1 : r_t(D_1) < r_t'(D_1')$.

However, from now on, $r_t(D_1)$ will be written as r_t for the sake of simplification of symbols except (iii) of proposition 2.

Proof (i) First, we will show that the sequence $\{r_t\}_{t=1}^{\infty}$ is monotonically decreasing. Let us verify the convergence of $\{r_t\}_{t=1}^{\infty}$. From the given preferences the market clearing condition is[12]

$$S_t^b(r_t) = 100(1 - 1/2r_t) = B_t/r_t.$$

Solve this equation for B_t,

$$B_t = 100(r_t - 1/2) \tag{A-4}$$

Substitute B_t into the temporary equilibrium condition (ii), we have a difference equation with respect to r_t.

$$r_{t+1} = 1/(3 - 2r_t) \tag{A-5}$$

Take the difference between r_{t+1} and r_t.

$$r_{t+1} - r_t = 1/(3 - 2r_t) - 1/(3 - 2r_{t-1})$$

$$= 2(r_t - r_{t-1})/(3 - 2r_t)(3 - 2r_{t-1})$$

Suppose $(3 - 2r_t)(3 - 2r_{t-1}) > 0$, then $r_{t+1} - r_t$ and $(r_t - r_{t-1})$ have the same sign. In the proof of lemma 1, we have that given $\forall B_1 \in (0, 50), \forall t \geq 1 : 0 < B_t < 50$ holds. By (A-1),

$$1/2 < r_t = B_t/100 + 1/2 < 1.$$

Then, by lemma 2 we have given $\forall D_1 \in (0, 50), \forall t \geq 1 : 1/2 < r_t < 1$. Therefore, $(3 - 2r_t)(3 - 2r_{t-1}) > 0$ holds.

Considering the initial period, by (A-5) we have

$$r_2 - r_1 = 1/(3 - 2r_1) - r_1 = (2r_1^2 - 3r_1 + 1)/(3 - 2r_1).$$

Since $1/2 < r_1 < 1$,

$$2r_1^2 - 3r_1 + 1 = (r_1 - 1)(2r_1 - 1) < 0.$$

[12] See definition 1 (temporary equilibrium).

We have $r_2 < r_1$. By mathematical induction, $\{r_t\}_{t+1}^{\infty}$ is monotonically decreasing. Since we have shown the sequence $\{r_t\}_{t+1}^{\infty}$ is bounded for $\forall B_1 \in (0, 50)$. By convergence of the theorem of bounded monotonic sequence, $\{r_t\}_{t=1}^{\infty}$ converges.

Now, take $r_t = r$ for $t \geq 1$ in (A-5).

$$2r^2 - 3r + 1 = 0$$

We have $r = 1, 1/2$. Since $\{r_t\}_{t=1}^{\infty}$ is monotonically decreasing, $\lim_{t\to\infty} r_t = 1/2$. ■

Proof (ii) Since $\forall t \geq 1 : B_t(0) = 0$ by corollary 2(i), when $D_1 = 0, \forall t \geq 1 : r_t = 1/2$ by (A-4). Similarly, since $\forall t \geq 1 : B_t(50) = 50$ by corollary 2(ii), when $D_1 = 50, \forall t \geq 1 : r_t = 1$ by (A-4). ■

Proof (iii) Let $\{r_t\}_{t=1}^{\infty}$ and $\{r_t'\}_{t=1}^{\infty}$ be respectively the sequences of the gross interest rates at the initial deficits D_1 and D_1' both of which satisfy the redeemable condition $0 < D_1 < D_1' < 50$. We will use the mathematical induction to prove this proposition. First, we will show that if $D_1 < D_1'$, then $r_1 < r_1'$. By the conditions of the temporary equilibrium conditions (i) and (iii),

$$S_1(r_1) = 100(1 - 1/2r_1) = B_1/r_1 = D_1$$

Solve this for r_1,

$$r_1 = 50/(100 - D_1)$$

Then, if $D_1 < D_1'$, then $r_1 < r_1'$ holds.

Suppose that when $t = k > 2$, $r_k < r_k'$ holds. By (A-5),

$$r_{k+1}' - r_{k+1}$$

$$= 1/(3 - 2r_k') - 1/(3 - 2r_k)$$

$$= 2(r_k' - r_k)/(3 - 2r_k')(3 - 2r_k)$$

By proof proposition 2 (i), we have shown when $\forall D_1 \in (0, 50), \forall t \geq 1 : 1/2 < r_t < 1$. Then

$$1 < 3 - 2r_k < 2$$

holds. Therefore, we have $r_{k+1} < r_{k+1}'$. ■

Now, we will prove the lemma 3 to show the welfare results in proposition 3.

Lemma 3 (i) *Let $c_{21}^h(D_1)$ be the consumption of the current old (a member h of generation 0 at period 1) given D_1. $c_{21}^h(D_1)$ increases as D_1 increases.*

(ii) *Let $u_t^h(D_1)$ be the utility of the young (a member h of generation $t \geq 1$) given D_1. $\forall D_1(0 < D_1 < 50) : \{u_t^h(D_1)\}_{t=1}^{\infty}$ is monotonically decreasing.*

(iii) $\forall D_1(0 < D_1 < 50) : \lim_{t\to\infty} u_t^h(D_1) = 2..$

Proof (i) The government decides the fiscal deficit, D_1 and distributes it equally among the old of a generation $h \in N_0$. Per-capita allocation for the initial old is defined as

$$d_1^h \stackrel{def}{\equiv} D_1/N_0$$

where the redeemable condition is $0 < D_1 < 50$. Then the consumption of the first period old is

$c_{21}^h(D_1) = w_{21}^h + d_1^h = 1 + D_1/100$ $(0 < D_1 < 50)$,
which means that $c_{21}^h(D_1)$ increases as D_1 increases. ■

Proof (ii) Cosider the sequence $\{u_t^h(D_1)\}_{t=1}^{\infty}$ subject to the redeemable condition $\forall D_1 \in (0, 50)$. In the temporary equilibrium, the consumption for the young is written as a function of r_t,

$$c_{1t}^h = w_{1t}^h/2 + w_{2,t+1}^h/2r_t = 1 + 1/2r_t.$$

Similarly, the consumption for the old is.
$c_{2,t+1}^h = w_{2,t+1}^h + r_t(w_{1t}^h/2 - w_{2,t+1}^h/2r_t) = 1/2 + r_t.$
Then, the utility for the young is written as a function of r_t,

$$u_t^h(D_1) = (1 + 1/2r_t)(1/2 + r_t) = 1 + 1/4r_t + r_t \tag{A-6}$$

Take the difference between the utilities for the young at period t and the young at period $t + 1$.

$$u_{t+1}^h(D_1) - u_t^h(D_1) = (1 + 1/4r_{t+1} + r_{t+1}) - (1 + 1/4r_t + r_t)$$

$$= (1 - 1/4r_{t+1}r_t)(r_{t+1} - r_t)$$

In the proof of proposition 2 (i), we have shown that the gross interest rate subject to the redeemable path satisfies the condition, $\forall t \geq 1 : 1/2 < r_t < 1$. Then we have.
$1 - 1/4r_{t+1}r_t > 0.$

Therefore, both $(u_{t+1}^h(D_1) - u_t^h(D_1))$ and $(r_{t+1} - r_t)$ have same sign. A sequence of $\{u_t^h(D_1)\}_{t=1}^{\infty}$ is monotonically decreasing since $\{r_t\}_{t=1}^{\infty}$ is monotonically decreasing.[13] ■

[13] See the proof of proposition 2 (i).

Proof (iii) By proposition 2 (i), we have $\forall D_1(0 < D_1 < 50) : \lim_{t\to\infty} r_t = 1/2$. Then, by (A-6), we have $\forall D_1(0 < D_1 < 50) : \lim_{t\to\infty} u_t^h(D_1) = 2$.

By (A-6), when $D_1 = 0, \forall t \geq 1 : u_t^h(0) = 2$ since when $D_1 = 0, \forall t \geq 1 :$ $r_t = 1/2$. Similarly, by (A-6), when $D_1 = 50, \forall t \geq 1 : u_t^h(50) = 2.25$ since when $D_1 = 50, \forall t \geq 1 : r_t = 1$. ■

Proposition 3 (i) *Eqm* $\{B_t(D_1)\}_{t=1}^{\infty}$ $(0 < D_1 < 50)$ *is sequential Pareto superior to Eqm* $\{B_t(0)\}_{t=1}^{\infty}$.

(ii) *Eqm* $\{B_t(50)\}_{t=1}^{\infty}$ *is sequential Pareto superior to Eqm* $\{B_t(D_1)\}_{t=1}^{\infty}$ *where* $0 < D_1 < 50$.

(iii) *Eqm* $\{B_t(50)\}_{t=1}^{\infty}$ *is sequential Pareto optimal.*

(iv) $\forall \mathrm{D}_1, \mathrm{D}_1'(0 < \mathrm{D}_1 < \mathrm{D}_1' < 50)$:*Eqm* $\{\mathrm{B}_t(\mathrm{D}_1')\}_{t=1}^{\infty}$ *is sequential Pareto superior to Eqm* $\{B_t(D_1)\}_{t=1}^{\infty}$.

(v) $\forall D_1 \in (0, 50)$ *and* $t < t' \Rightarrow$ *Eqm* $B_t(D_1)$ *is sequential Pareto superior to Eqm* $B_{t'}(D_1)$.[14]

Proof (i) The consumption allocation of status quo, Eqm $\{B_t(0)\}_{t=1}^{\infty}$ is $\{c_{21}^h(0) = 1 \text{ for } h \in N_0, (c_{1t}^h, c_{2t}^h) = (2, 1) \text{ for } h \in N_t\}_{t=1}^{\infty}$. The consumption for the old which is equivalent to the utility is $c_{21}^h(0) = 1$ for $\forall h \in N_0$ and the utility of the young is $\{u_t^h(0)\}_{t=1}^{\infty} = \{2\}_{t=1}^{\infty}$ for $\forall h \in N_t$. On the other hand, in the path of redeemable process, Eqm $\{B_t(D_1)\}_{t=1}^{\infty}$ $(0 < D_1 < 50)$, the consumption for the old is $c_{21}^h(D_1) = 1 + d_1 > 1$ $(d_1 \overset{def}{\equiv} D_1/N_1)$ and the sequence of the utility for the young is $\{u_t^h(D_1)\}_{t=1}^{\infty}$ is monotonically decreasing and converges to 2 by lemma 3 (ii) and (iii). Therefore, any redeemable sequence of temporary equilibrium, Eqm $\{B_t(D_1)\}_{t=1}^{\infty}$ $(0 < D_1 < 50)$ is sequential Pareto superior to the status quo, Eqm $\{B_t(0)\}_{t=1}^{\infty}$. ■

Proof (ii) The consumption allocation of the stationary state is Eqm $\{B_t(50)\}_{t=1}^{\infty}$ is $\{c_{21}^h(50) = 3/2 \text{ for } h \in N_0, (c_{1t}^h, c_{2t}^h) = (3/2, 3/2) \text{ for } h \in N_t\}_{t=1}^{\infty}$. The utility for the old which is equivalent to the consumption is $c_{21}^h(50) = 3/2$ for $\forall h \in N_0$ and the utility of the young is $\{u_t^h(50)\}_{t=1}^{\infty} = \{2.25\}_{t=1}^{\infty}$ for $\forall h \in N_t$. On the other hand, in the path of redeemable process, Eqm $\{B_t(D_1)\}_{t=1}^{\infty}$ $(0 < D_1 < 50)$, the consumption for the old is $c_{21}^h(D_1) = 1 + d_1 < 3/2$ $(d_1 \overset{def}{\equiv} D_1/N_1)$ and the sequence of the utility for the young is $\{u_t^h(D_1)\}_{t=1}^{\infty}$ is monotonically decreasing by lemma 3 (ii). Eqm $\{B_t(50)\}_{t=1}^{\infty}$ is sequential Pareto superior to any Eqm $\{B_t(D_1)\}_{t=1}^{\infty}$ $(0 < D_1 < 50)$. ■

Proof (iii) By propositions (i) and (ii), there does not exist any sequences which is sequential Pareto superior to Eqm $\{B_t(50)\}_{t=1}^{\infty}$ for $D_1 \in [0, 50)$. ■

---

14 $\mathrm{Eq}^m\, B_t(D_1)$ is defined as the competitive equilibrium at period t as an element of the sequence of the temporary equilibrium.

Proof (iv) Take any D_1 and $D_1'(0 < D_1 < D_1' < 50)$ both of which create redeemable sequence. The consumptions of the old are

$$\text{when } D_1 < D_1', c_{21}^h(D_1) < c_{21}^h(D_1')$$

where

$$c_{21}^h(D_1) = 1 + d_1\left(d_1 \overset{\text{def}}{\equiv} D_1/N_0\right).$$

Now, suppose that the government decides the fiscal deficits D_1 at the first period, the sequence of utilities is

$$u_t^h(D_1) = 1 + 1/4r_t + r_t.$$

Take the difference between the sequences of utilities under D_1' and D_1.

$$u_t^h(D_1') - u_t^h(D_1) = 1/4r_t' - 1/4r_t + r_t' - r_t$$

$$= (1 - 1/4r_t'r_t)(r_t' - r_t) \tag{A-7}$$

By proposition 2 (i), we have

$$\forall t \geq 1 : 1/2 < r_t < 1 \text{ when } D_1 \in (0, 50).$$

The first term of r.h.s. of (A-7) is positive. By proposition 2 (iii), we have

$$\forall t \geq 1 : r_t < r_t' \text{ when } D_1 < D_1'.$$

The second term of r.h.s. of (A-7) is positive. Therefore, r.h.s. of (A-7) is positive and we get the result.

$$\forall t \geq 1 : u_t^h(D_1) < u_t^h(D_1') \text{ when } D_1 < D_1'.$$

■

Proof (v) Take any redeemable sequence and choose temporary equilibrium at period t and period t' where $t < t'$. By lemma 3 (ii), we have shown that $\{u_t^h(D_1)\}_{t=1}^{\infty}$ is monotonically decreasing, when $t < t'$, $u_t^h(D_1) > u_{t'}^h(D_1)$. ■

Proposition 4 *Consider two sequences of government policy,* $\{D_t\}_{t=1}^{\infty} = \{D_1, 0, \cdots\}$ *and* $\{D_t\}_{t=1}^{\infty} = \{D_1, 0, \cdots, 0, D_k, 0, \cdots\}$ *both of which satisfy the redeemable condition. The latter allocation is sequential Pareto superior to the former allocation.*

Proof Both allocations have the same sequence until period $k-1$. After period k, the allocations are realized under the sequences of the government bonds, $\{B_t(D_1)\}_{t=k}^{\infty}$ and $\{B_t(D_1, D_k)\}_{t=k}^{\infty}$ such that

$$B_t(D_1) < B_t(D_1, D_k).$$

By lemma 2 and proposition 3 (iv), the temporary equilibrium under $\{B_t(D_1, D_k)\}_{t=k}^{\infty}$ is Pareto superior to the temporary equilibrium under $\{B_t(D_1)\}_{t=k}^{\infty}$. Therefore, in the case of the whole sequence for $t \geq 1$, the temporary equilibrium under $\{B_k(D_1, D_k)\}_{t=1}^{\infty}$ is Pareto superior to the temporary equilibrium under $\{B_k(D_1)\}_{t=1}^{\infty}$. ■

References

Blanchard, Olivier. 2019. Public Debt and Low Interest Rates. American Economic Review 2019, 109(4): 1197–1229

Sims, A. Christopher. 2013. Paper Money. American Economic Review. 103(2): 563–584

Chapter 7
Conclusion

Abstract This paper has presented three questions about the Japanese economic policy and provided answers from the perspective of standard macro theory. The impact of fiscal policy on prices (Question 1) and the macro analysis of MMT (Question 2) are conducted by the mechanism by which government bonds are settled on the monetary base. On the other hand, in the answer to Question 3, public debt is analyzed on the assumption that government bonds and the monetary base are the same. However, government bonds are IOUs that do not have finality while the monetary base issued by the central bank have finality. Therefore, from the viewpoint of the economics of payments, the analysis of public debt by distinguishing between government bonds and the monetary base will be an issue for the future.

In the first half of this research, we summarized and evaluated the conduct of economic policy to date by explaining the Japanese economy from the perspective of fiscal deficits and deflation. We described the results of deflationary countermeasures implemented under excessive public debts and the reasons why the price stability target of 2 percent could not be achieved. Deflation caused by the bursting of the asset bubble in 1990, manifested itself between 1997 and 1998, and the Bank faced the problem of "zero lower bound" in the conventional monetary easing policy. Once short-term interest rates reached zero, there was no further monetary easing policy at the time. Therefore, the Bank was forced to seek an unconventional monetary policy. The time duration policy introduced by the zero-interest rate policy in 1998 and the quantitative easing policy (QE) in 2001 led to the new monetary management tool as forward guidance since the global financial crisis. It was an operating conduct that considered the effect of the commitment to continue monetary easing until the target was achieved. Quantitative and Qualitative Monetary Easing (QQE) evolved from this policy experience consists of the operating targets of interest rate control by massive purchases of JGBs and inflation expectations. As a result of the policy experiments, the knowledge that the shape of the yield curve could be controlled by massive purchase of short and long-term JGBs was gained, but inflation expectations did not work. The reason is that the forward-looking component, which is the impetus of inflation expectations, did not function because it has been anchored

Y. Sakai, *Deflation and Fiscal Deficits*, SpringerBriefs in Economics,
https://doi.org/10.1007/978-981-97-0415-6_7

to deflation mind by the backward-looking component. On the other hand, QQE, which initially performed well, suffered a setback after the consumption tax hike in 2014. This was the incident in which fiscal policy undermined the operating target of monetary policy.

These facts suggest that monetary policy is meant to provide an environment that facilitates borrowing, not a means of physically increasing the money stock. This is because credit creation, which connects the monetary base and the money stock, is supported by voluntary activities of financial institutions in response to private demand for funds.[1] As explained in Figs. 3.2 and 3.3, the series of monetary policies in Japan was to induce a spontaneous increase in the money stock through the huge supply of the monetary base. In the circumstance where a deflationary gap has occurred, it has been recognized from the experience so far that monetary policy alone cannot raise prices unless inflation expectations work effectively. Therefore, it is necessary to directly increase the money stock through fiscal policy.

In the second half of the research, we tried to give a solution to what economic measures can be taken based on the findings we obtained so far. We consider the fiscal theory of the price level (FTPL) as an alternative to inflation expectations. If QQE cannot work when credit creation does not function, FTPL gives us the brilliant idea of a mechanism to artificially withdraw the money stock instead of the monetary base. It is an attempt to derive a mechanism to explain the relationship between the government expenditure and prices. As one of such mechanisms, we constructed a macro model that incorporates the financial institutions to clarify transactions between the public sector and the private sector. Figure 5.2 describes the price determination mechanism in which fiscal and monetary policies are interdependent. In particular, the central bank provides the services of current accounts among the financial institutions and the government. We derive a mechanism by which fiscal policy determines prices in a framework that incorporated the financial institutions into the private sector. In it, for government bonds to be redeemed and the money stock to increase, the monetary base must be unlimitedly provided by the central bank. Then the government expenditure can function as a means of actively increasing the money stock itself. Rather than conducting independently fiscal and monetary policies for the soundness of public debt and price stability, the government and the central bank operate their targets under a single unified system. Through the transaction mechanism constructed here, the relationship between fiscal spending and prices can be more clearly understood.

Next, we theoretically described the modern monetary theory (MMT) proposition that "public debt is the wealth of the state" under the action of the government called S(BAT). We have derived the observation of MMT (see Figs. 5.4 and 5.6) from the mechanism of FTPL (see Figs. 5.3 and 5.5). It suggests the MMT assertion is not

[1] On the other hand, monetary policy is considered effective in case where inflation expectations are sufficiently high, because monetary tightening through interest rates can directly affect credit creation. For example, the facts that the first oil shock (1973–1977) was brought under control in a short period of time and that it had a strong effect on countermeasures against the bubble in the early 1990s suggests that the tightening policy was effective. These experiences suggest an asymmetry exists in the mechanism of monetary policy between in dealing with the cases deflation and inflation.

theoretically contradictory with the standard macro-economic model. It is also shown S(TAB) is supported by fiscal financing.

In previous discussions, we have explained the relationship between fiscal spending and prices. In a Japan with huge budget deficits, government spending is equivalent to public debt. The remaining problem, therefore, is the relationship between public debt and financial collapse. As an answer to Question 3, we presented a model to consistently explain both the crocodile mouth theory and Blanchard's assertion. We have presented a model describing both a case that leads to a financial collapse when the fiscal deficit becomes enormous and a case in which further fiscal spending increases economic efficiency when public debt can be repaid by refinancing. If there is a threshold for public debt and exceeding it will lead to a financial collapse, the crocodile mouth theory holds, while if it is within the threshold, new issues of government bond will be repeated. In addition, Blanchard claims that an increase in public debt contributes to economic welfare. Our model shows the property that an economy in the process of paying off public debt tends to be less efficient. Namely, as a result, there is a threshold to public debt as to the financial collapse, but the efficiency increases if public debt is increased by fiscal policy. To enable such proposition to hold, we have considered the sequence of temporary equilibria and adopted the sequential Pareto optimality in the intertemporal economics.

Finally, we would like to touch on the assumption of homogeneity between the monetary base and government bonds. The answer to Question 3 is established on the premise that government bonds and central bank currencies are identical. How should we think about the equivalence between government bonds and the monetary base? Government bonds are securities issued as IOU by a country, and the monetary base is securities issued by the central bank. The monetary base has the function of finality which means to complete an economic transaction by way of paying for it, but government bonds do not retain such one. In other words, government bonds do not have a function of medium of exchange, nor as a measure of value. We should also consider demand deposits supplied by the financial institutions as a currency with finality. This is a reason we have focused on the financial institutions and current accounts at central bank in the answer to Question 1. In the answer to Question 3, the distinction between the government bonds and the monetary base is replaced with the homogeneity among them because government bonds are refinanced by an unlimited supply of central bank currency. The problem on this point belongs to the economics of payments, Freeman (1996) and the model of consolidated budget constraints, Sargent (2013) as future research.

References

Freeman, Scott. 1996. "The payment system, liquidity, and rediscounting," American Economic Review, Vol. 86, 1126–38.

Sargent, Thomas. 2013. Rational Expectations and Inflation. 3rd ed. Princeton University Press. Some Unpleasant Monetarist Arithmetic with Neil Wallace.

GPSR Compliance
The European Union's (EU) General Product Safety Regulation (GPSR) is a set of rules that requires consumer products to be safe and our obligations to ensure this.

If you have any concerns about our products, you can contact us on

ProductSafety@springernature.com

In case Publisher is established outside the EU, the EU authorized representative is:

Springer Nature Customer Service Center GmbH
Europaplatz 3
69115 Heidelberg, Germany

www.ingramcontent.com/pod-product-compliance
Ingram Content Group UK Ltd.
Pitfield, Milton Keynes, MK11 3LW, UK
UKHW020704041026
15590UKWH00001B/455
* 9 7 8 9 8 1 9 7 0 4 1 4 9 *